GEORGE SAND AND AUTOBIOGRAPHY

THE EUROPEAN HUMANITIES RESEARCH CENTRE

UNIVERSITY OF OXFORD

The European Humanities Research Centre of the University of Oxford organizes a range of academic activities, including conferences and workshops, and publishes scholarly works under its own imprint, LEGENDA. Within Oxford, the EHRC bridges, at the research level, the main humanities faculties: Modern Languages, English, Modern History, Literae Humaniores, Music and Theology. The Centre stimulates interdisciplinary research collaboration throughout these subject areas and provides an Oxford base for advanced researchers in the humanities.

The Centre's publications programme focuses on making available the results of advanced research in medieval and modern languages and related interdisciplinary areas. An Editorial Board, whose members are drawn from across the British university system, covers the principal European languages. Titles include works on French, German, Italian, Portuguese, Russian and Spanish literature. In addition, the EHRC co-publishes with the Society for French Studies, the British Comparative Literature Association and the Modern Humanities Research Association. The Centre also publishes *Oxford German Studies* and *Film Studies*, and has launched a Special Lecture Series under the LEGENDA imprint.

Enquiries about the Centre's publishing activities should be addressed to:
Professor Malcolm Bowie, Director

Further information:
Kareni Bannister, Senior Publications Officer
European Humanities Research Centre
University of Oxford
47 Wellington Square, Oxford OX1 2JF
enquiries@ehrc.ox.ac.uk
www.ehrc.ox.ac.uk

LEGENDA

LEGENDA

EUROPEAN HUMANITIES RESEARCH CENTRE
RESEARCH MONOGRAPHS IN FRENCH STUDIES 5

Frontispiece: Portrait of George Sand by Nadar, 1864
Photo: AKG London

George Sand and Autobiography

JANET HIDDLESTON

LEGENDA

European Humanities Research Centre
University of Oxford
Research Monographs in French Studies 5
1999

Published for the Society for French Studies by the
European Humanities Research Centre
of the University of Oxford
47 Wellington Square
Oxford OX1 2JF

LEGENDA is the publications imprint of the
European Humanities Research Centre

ISBN 1 900755 25 4
ISSN 1466-8157

First published 1999

British Library Cataloguing in Publication Data
A CIP catalogue record for this book is available from the British Library

© European Humanities Research Centre of the University of Oxford 1999

LEGENDA series designed by Cox Design Partnership, Witney, Oxon
Printed in Great Britain by
Information Press
Eynsham
Oxford OX8 1JJ

Chief Copy-Editor: Genevieve Hawkins

CONTENTS

FOR JIM
AND FOR OUR FOUR DAUGHTERS

INTRODUCTION

I

The most important text left us by George Sand could be said to be her life, for until recently it is certainly her life that has attracted most attention. In the last twenty years, however, with the increasing interest in her hitherto neglected writings, the text of that 'text' which is her autobiography has also attracted attention, not just as a source for the many stories of her life written by others but as a work in its own right with its own story to tell.

The growing popularity of Sand, the increasing number of studies devoted to her work, have of course been the result of the emergence of women's writing as a separate discipline, and the context in which her works have most often been considered has been a feminist one. Questions of gender have dominated, so that her early novels, for example, have most often been read in Freudian terms and her later socialism has been seen to take a peculiarly feminine form. Yet of all her writings, it is perhaps to her autobiography, the *Histoire de ma vie*, that her gender is most relevant since an autobiography depends much more directly for its material on the actual person of the autobiographer to whose construction gender is fundamental.

For Sand, the question of gender was a particularly tricky one; indeed much of our fascination with her stems from her sexual ambiguity. Her early life had encouraged in her an uncertainty about her sexuality which was later followed by a defiant adoption of a masculine way of life as an independent, professional writer of social and religious fiction as well as of the 'sentimental' novels more usually expected of a woman. At the same time, she cherished the feminine arts of needlework and cookery, and was a devoted if often absent mother. She aroused strong feelings in her contemporaries. Baudelaire abused her, it seems, for her very femininity: 'Elle est bête, elle est lourde, elle est bavarde; elle a dans les idées morales la même profondeur de jugement et la même délicatesse de sentiment que les concierges et les filles entretenues.'[1] Vigny emphasized her manliness: 'Sans grâce dans le maintien, rude dans le parler. Homme dans la tournure, le langage, le son de la voix et la hardiesse des expressions'.[2] Others saw in her the best of both sexes, Balzac for example describing her thus: 'Elle est garçon, elle est artiste, elle est grande, généreuse, dévouée, *chaste*, elle a les grands traits de l'homme, *ergo* elle n'est pas femme',[3] and Flaubert writing of her shortly after her death: 'Il fallait la connaître comme je l'ai connue pour savoir tout ce qu'il y avait de féminin dans ce grand homme, l'immensité de tendresse qui se trouvait dans ce génie.'[4]

She talked often of the irrelevance for her of gender boundaries, referring to herself in the masculine, and writing to Adolphe Guéroult in 1835: 'Prenez-moi donc pour un homme ou une femme, comme vous voudrez. Duteil dit que je ne suis ni l'un ni l'autre mais que je suis un être';[5] and towards the end of her life, in a letter to Flaubert, she claimed: '*Il n'y a qu'un sexe*. Un homme et une femme c'est si bien la même chose que l'on ne comprend guère les tas de distinctions et de raisonnements subtils dont se sont nourries les sociétés sur ce chapitre-là.'[6] There was much contemporary interest in the liberating potential of the androgynous figure, and some writers experimented with its different incarnations in their fiction—Balzac in *Séraphita* and Gautier in *Mademoiselle de Maupin*, for example. Sand too invented characters who were both female and male: Gabriel, who is taken to be a man, and Edmée, a beautiful woman with the will and intelligence of a man, are among the most obvious. Sand, however, is alone in attempting to realize such possibilities in her own person and her own life.[7]

Questions of gender definition have particular interest in a discussion of autobiography since with the rise of autobiographical theory, such discussion has become increasingly gender-specific. It is only in the last thirty years that autobiography has been seen as a literary genre at all, with its own conventions and expectations, and has inspired its own theorization. With the publication of a large number of studies, both theoretical and textual, a body of theory has gradually emerged:[8] the emphasis has shifted from the past life, to the present self that lived the life, to the written text of that self's life. An autobiography has come to be seen as more revealing of its narrator than of his younger self because of the ways in which he chooses to tell his story. The autobiographical project itself and the relation between autobiographer and reader are now thought to be crucially defining. Emphasis is also placed on the self-referring and circular conventionality of writing itself until, for Paul de Man for example, the actual person doing the writing has almost disappeared: 'Autobiography, then, is not a genre or a mode, but a figure of reading or of understanding that occurs, to some degree, in all texts.'[9]

In the early 1980s, a second category of autobiography emerged.[10] Autobiographies by women were seen to be different from those by men, fragmented and digressive instead of linear, concerned with the private and personal rather than the public and political, although also necessarily depicting the difficult conquest of the female self and the achieving of recognition against all the odds. Women were said to discover themselves with and through rather than against other people, the relationship of the daughter with her mother being central.

Needless to say, in all these largely theoretical studies, Sand's *Histoire de ma vie* is scarcely mentioned. Indeed, for many years, all Sand's writings were thoroughly out of fashion, too feminist for some, not feminist enough for others. Idealist rather than realist, seen as garrulous as well as prolific, she survived largely as the writer of rural novels which were seen, by Proust's mother among others, as stories for children. Since her tempestuous life had continued to fascinate, her autobiography was still read as a source of information but assessed only for its accuracy, and so most often dismissed as simplistic and idealizing. Picon calls it 'le plus romanesque de ses romans',[11] and Pierre Salomon in his biography accuses her of replacing the woman she was with the woman she would like to have been.[12] Its unreliability as a record of her life is linked by Henry James to the fact that she was a woman and therefore bound to lie: 'There is something very liberal and universal in George Sand's genius, as well as very masculine; but our final impression of her always is that she is a woman and a Frenchwoman. Women, we are told, do not value the truth for its own sake, but only for some personal use they make of it.'[13] Thus, while admiring her person and many of her novels, he describes the *Histoire* as 'a nondescript performance, which has neither the value of truth nor the illusion of fiction',[14] with 'its odd mixture of the didactic and the irresponsible'.[15]

If we look at Sand's autobiography however, not as a straight account of her life, but in terms of the autobiographical theory outlined above, our assessment may be rather different. Indeed, given her ambiguous sexual positioning, a reading from the perspective of gender may be a particularly fruitful one; and, beginning with Helene Deutsch in 1946,[16] almost all the important articles on the *Histoire* this century interpret it from a heavily Freudian perspective, tracing for example the relative importance of Sand's early relationship with her father and/or mother for her subsequent development. These studies will be discussed at length in Chapter 2. Other critics have attempted to set the *Histoire de ma vie* within the context of the genre, in particular by reference to Rousseau's *Confessions*, so as to estimate her place in the overall tradition,[17] and Nancy Miller in a brief discussion of women's autobiography in France has linked her with Daniel Stern and Colette.[18]

I hope to include all these perspectives in a fuller study of the *Histoire*, which will discuss the text from the point of view of structure and style as well as content, making as much of the way the self-conscious narrator chooses, consciously or unconsciously, to present her younger self as of the changing nature of that younger self. At each point, I shall assess the extent to which this hybrid, androgynous text follows the conventions of the traditional (male) autobiography and how far its differences can be attributed to the fact that Sand was a woman. One result may be to make us wary of any over-simple polarization according to gender; another, I hope, will be to illuminate further the complexities of her own sexual disposition and thus gain a more intimate access to her person.

2

How did Sand herself see her autobiography? In what context did she write it and with what purpose? She began the *Histoire de ma vie* in 1847 and continued it with interruptions until 1854 when it was published in instalments between September 1854 and August 1855. Although her initial reason for writing was to earn money for her daughter's dowry, she had also arrived at a time of life when it was not uncommon for public figures, writers in particular, to undertake the composition of their memoirs; Stendhal and Chateaubriand are among the most celebrated to have done so at about the same time. A crucial factor in this development was undoubtedly the publication in 1782 of Rousseau's *Confessions*, seen as a kind of benchmark by all subsequent autobiographers including Sand. Indeed, Roy Pascal defines as central to the history of autobiography the years between

1782 and 1831, the date of Goethe's *Poetry and Truth*.[19] This was the time, he argues, when the genre came to full consciousness and finally took shape, with the result that more and more autobiographies began to be written. To the confessional aim of the earlier spiritual autobiographies and the humanist individualism of the Renaissance and the Enlightenment was added the Romantic delight in introspection and its privileging of childhood as the key to adult life. Also influential was the proliferation in the eighteenth century of fictional autobiographical texts in the form of memoir, diary and letter novels, leading to a certain blurring of the distinction between fact and fiction which inevitably contaminated autobiography proper.

Although the most famous of these texts, whether fictional or directly autobiographical, were by men—Marivaux, Prévost, Rousseau or Laclos (often though with a woman as main protagonist)—we have become increasingly aware of a wealth of material published by women too at this time and avidly read by its public. The literary salons of the eighteenth century, presided over by women, provided a milieu and attitude of mind which allowed them to write, whether or not they were actually members of a salon. Moreover, the sentimental subject matter of such works, their exploration of the private lives of men and women in their relationships with each other, seemed to be particularly suited to a woman's pen since it lay directly within her experience of life. The list of names is a long one—Madame de Tencin, Madame de Charrières, Madame de Graffigny, Madame Riccoboni and, most famously at the end of the century, Madame de Staël, who also produced what one might call more male texts, on politics and culture.

Writing one's own life-story rather than that of a fictional character was perhaps more difficult for women, even in this relatively favourable time, since such a project implied a self-confidence and even a presumption which could be thought unfeminine, as well as a certain celebrity and experience of public life. Such female narratives had earlier been legitimized by being religious, like the Life of St Teresa of Avila, for example, or Julian of Norwich in England. Madame Roland was drawn to put pen to paper in her memoirs of 1793 only in order to justify her life from the prison in which she was held during the Revolution; she states clearly that in no other circumstances would she have been induced to write for publication: 'Jamais je n'eus la plus légère tentation de devenir auteur un jour; je vis de très bonne heure qu'une femme qui gagnait ce titre perdait beaucoup plus qu'elle n'avait acquis',[20] suggesting that some stigma still attached to the profession of authoress.

The stigma was no doubt felt even more acutely as life became harder for ambitious and independent women after the Revolution. With the break-up of the Ancien Régime the salons had largely disappeared, and this, together with the repressive effect of the Napoleonic code,[21] allowed no space, no context for the woman writer: 'To be a woman writer in nineteenth-century France meant being outside the mainstream.'[22] Some of course were undaunted and carried on writing anyway, out of financial necessity or driven by a more profound urge to express themselves—Hortense Allart and Daniel Stern (pseudonym of Marie d'Agoult), for example, whom Sand knew but from whom she kept her distance, and Flora Tristan with whose active political feminism she was very much out of sympathy. Indeed, both Flora Tristan and Daniel Stern wrote autobiographies as well as fiction, Tristan in 1838 under the cover of a description of a journey to Peru, and Stern in 1867–8, in a more conventional form, perhaps influenced by Sand's *Histoire* which she had certainly read. Tristan did briefly attain a certain scandalous notoriety for her political activities as much as for her writings, but none of these women came close to achieving Sand's success; for with the publication of *Indiana* in 1832, a year after her arrival in Paris, at the age of 26, Sand had taken the literary world by storm and immediately become central to French literary life. In spite of every difficulty, she had triumphantly created her own space, her own place, apparently unconfined by gender, neither male nor female but both at once and transcending both, androgynous; and it is from this space that the *Histoire de ma vie* was written.

Sand never saw herself as a woman writer. She set herself firmly within a male tradition: Hugo and Balzac were the main influences on her early novels and Rousseau is the master she claims for her autobiography. She rarely mentions Madame de Staël; when she refers to her *Réflexions sur le suicide* in the fourth *Lettre d'un voyageur*, her praise is no more than lukewarm: it is 'un écrit correct, logique, commun quant aux pensées, beau quant au style, et savant quant à l'arrangement' (II, 752).[23] In the *Histoire* she describes her lasting affection for the stories of Madame de Genlis but largely because they were read to her as a child by her mother in front of the fire. The writers she most admires and who had the greatest influence on her are Montaigne, Rousseau and Chateaubriand. It is in their wake that she is writing, philosophy and politics as well as fiction and memoirs, and it is against them that she asks to be judged.

In the twenty years between 1827 and 1848, she produced a series of autobiographical works, often under the cover of travel narratives but using forms that are patently autobiographical—diaries, letters and memoirs.[24] The link between travel and introspection goes back to Rousseau's *Rêveries d'un promeneur solitaire*, from whom derives the Romantic cliché of the solitary wanderer. Displacement in space leads to a liberation and also a disorientation highly conducive to self-contemplation, often leading to melancholy as well as elation. Sand's first substantial text of this kind is the *Voyage en Auvergne*, written in 1827 when she was 23, at the request of her friend, Jane Bazouin, but also as a response to the boredom she felt in her new environment (in spite of the presence of her husband and small son). It is a strange, fragmented work, written as a diary in a variety of tones, suggesting that its author is experimenting with a number of different voices as a diversion from her *ennui*. In amongst the humorous accounts of her travel companions, the witty dialogues she invented for them, and the self-consciously poetic descriptions of nature, thoughts of her mother and her despair at having been abandoned by her keep resurfacing. Indeed, it is the desire to write her a letter that triggers the entire text: 'Me voilà bien! si j'écrivais à quelqu'un? oui, à ma mère, par exemple! à ma mère, ah Dieu! "O, ma mère, que vous ai-je fait? pourquoi ne m'aimez-vous pas ..."' (II, 504). This anguish leads straight into a project for an autobiography with its different sections spelt out, which strangely prefigures the later *Histoire de ma vie* but is written now in a blunt, matter-of-fact tone which reverts quickly to the flippancy of the daily diary with which the text had started. It is perhaps these rapid shifts of mood themselves, the self-consciousness and irreverence even about her own despair which give the reader the strongest sense of the young woman's restlessnesss and depression at this time in her life. The autobiographical voice emerges indirectly, in spite of itself, and with none of the stability and self-confidence of the mature George Sand.

In her next autobiographical work, the twelve *Lettres d'un voyageur*, written between 1834 and 1836, partly to various friends and partly for publication, multiplicity becomes the guiding principle of the text. Sand speaks variously as a young student, an old man, a pilgrim, a poet, a solitary traveller, always in the masculine, as a way of freeing herself from the constraints of real life and disguising the true reasons for her suffering. As she puts it in the *Histoire*: 'je voulais faire le propre roman de ma vie et n'en être pas le personnage réel, mais le personnage pensant et analysant' (II, 299), and again in the Preface to the second edition she describes herself as 'parlant tantôt comme un écolier vagabond, tantôt comme un vieux oncle podagre, tantôt comme un jeune soldat impatient' (II, 646). Oddly, though, at various points in the letters she also appears as George Sand, recognizably herself: she is small in stature (letter 1), she has two children called Maurice and Solange (letter 3), she has written a novel called *Lélia* (letter 4), has lived in the Vallée noire (letter 7), is engaged in legal proceedings against her husband (letter 9), and finally talks directly as the author of her own works in letter 12. Of course these shifts in voice, these movements back and forth between different personae reflect Sand's changing moods and preoccupations in the years 1834–6. Embedded in the text, even if carefully disguised, are memories of the affair with Musset in Venice and the suicidal despair caused by its end; this is followed in letter 6 by the renewal of hope associated with her acquaintance with Michel de Bourges alongside the anxiety of the separation proceedings with her husband, and the work culminates in an open defence of her views and writings in letter 12 to Nisard. There are literal journeys—in Northern Italy, back to Nohant, to Switzerland and Paris—but more importantly we follow her mental journey from uncertainty and pessimism to optimism and self-confidence.[25] Yet the reader still feels strangely detached from the text, sharing little in the emotional experiences of the real person; we are momentarily convinced of her love of nature, her despair at separation or her delight in solitude, but the voices she adopts are too various and conflicting, the meditations too self-conscious, the rhetoric too studied for the work to be truly autobiographical. The intention seems to be more one of literary experimentation and display than of genuine self-exploration.

We have only to read the title of *Entretiens journaliers avec le très docte et très habile docteur Piffoël, professeur de botanique et de psychologie* to see how far we still are from a unified and authentic narrative voice. This brief, playful text takes the form of a diary of Sand's journey in Switzerland in 1837 with Liszt and Marie d'Agoult, on which she comments in a series of conversations she holds with herself in the guise of the venerable doctor Piffoël (so called because of Sand's large nose). Although her melancholy comes through, the work also captures well the holiday humour of the troop of friends, and it is difficult to take seriously as an enlightening autobiographical text.

Un hiver à Majorque, an account of the few months Sand spent in Majorca with Chopin and her two children in the winter of 1838–9, although not written until three years later, comes closest to being a traditional 'récit de voyage', from which we learn even less of the person of its author, although for different reasons. Her aim here was quite genuinely to give a full and objective description of the island, including its history, geography, landscapes and architecture, using her own personal experiences simply as a way in: 'Je prie donc ce dernier [the reader] de regarder ici ma personnalité comme une chose toute passive, comme une lunette d'approche à travers laquelle il pourra regarder ce qui se passe en ces pays lointains' (II, 1052). The picture of Majorca and its inhabitants that emerges is not entirely flattering. Although the majestic mountain scenery and the isolation of the family's life there (they had set up house in the half-ruined Charterhouse of Valldemosa) should have been conducive to nostalgia and introspection, the material conditions were so difficult that Sand had no time for reverie or self-recollection, and the narrative resolutely turns outward—to talk of leaking roofs, uneatable food and grasping natives rather than of solitary fantasies and Romantic wanderings. We learn nothing of Sand's feelings for Chopin; he is simply a delicate and musical friend for whom she has to provide as she does for her children. We do gather something of her courage and resourcefulness both from her ability to make the best of things while she was there, and also from the largely uncomplaining, matter-of-fact tone in which the text is written, but this is incidental rather than central and personal references are even further disguised by her continual speaking of herself in the masculine.

Although, then, the autobiographical impulse was present from early on, it was constantly obscured and displaced into other kinds of writing, which allowed Sand to speak as someone else. Many readers have felt better informed by her novels where she could more freely reveal the intimate aspects of her personality. Kathryn Crecelius interprets the early fiction largely in terms of Sand's own marital dreams and disappointments,[26] and the recurrence of doubles in her novels has also been linked to her childhood conflicts.[27] Naomi Schor makes a clear identification between the young Sand and 'la petite Fadette', both independent-minded, motherless tomboys, living a country life in the Berry.[28] Her contemporaries were in no doubt that she used the voice of Lélia to express her own anguish in a female version of the Romantic *mal du siècle*, and she admitted that there was something of herself in all the characters of the book (II, 615). The heroine of *Consuelo* bears some resemblance to how she may have seen herself: small, dark, plain, motherless and unconventional, at one point she spends several months dressed as a man, later becomes a celebrated artist (a singer), then finally joins a mystic brotherhood dedicated to an obscure belief in eternal human progress. In the *Histoire*, though, Sand denies any such resemblances, making a clear distinction between the romantic fantasies of fiction and the banality of fact: 'je ne me suis jamais mise en scène sous des traits féminins. Je suis trop romanesque pour avoir vu une héroïne de roman dans mon miroir' (II, 160).

Be that as it may, our present concern is not with Sand's fiction, however autobiographical, but with the one text that she presents directly as fact, with her autobiography proper, the *Histoire de ma vie*. It was only in 1847, six years after *Un hiver à Majorque*, at the age of 43, that she finally addressed the reader openly and publicly as herself in order to give a conventionally retrospective, chronological account of her life, the life of the young Amantine-Lucile-Aurore Dupin/Dudevant who had become George Sand. She was writing now as the established professional author and well-respected owner and benefactor of Nohant, where she was permanently settled after her bohemian years in Paris and the scandal of her many love affairs. She was anxious to put the record straight, to present herself as respectable and worldly-wise. She had achieved the independent life she wanted and did not want to shock, either through her life or through her works. She wished to remain within the mainstream, to confirm her reputation as a central literary figure, not to draw attention to her (sexual) difference. Thus the narrative structures she uses seem conventional and unsurprising, the tone in which she writes generally detached, apparently asexual, almost bland. Although she is necessarily concerned with the life of a girl and young woman in nineteenth-century France whose experiences were perforce different from those of a man, she makes little of this difference and offers herself as typical of all humankind. Indeed, Thelma Jurgrau feels the need to create 'A third category of autobiography, as yet uninvented [...] to contain [...] the neutral tranquillity that dominates the telling of her story, that neither men's nor women's auto-biographies typically contain'.[29] So any specificity according to gender is removed.

And yet, can it really be so easy? However liberated Sand felt herself to be from the limitations of her sex, she had suffered from them in her youth; they were part of her story and had made her what she was. Perhaps we should not take her narrative entirely at face value, but read it rather as Gilbert and Gubar read the great English women novelists of the nineteenth century and show how, like them, Sand revised the 'male genres, using them to record their own dreams and their own stories *in disguise*'.[30] Quoting Elizabeth Barrett Browning's two poems on Sand, one in which she is described partly as a man and the other as a woman, Gilbert and Gubar point out the difficulties of her ambivalent position: 'For a woman artist is, after all, a woman—that is her "problem"—and if she denies her own gender she inevitably confronts an identity crisis as severe as the anxiety of authorship she is trying to surmount.'[31] They see her as 'not wholesomely androgynous but unhealthily hermaphroditic',[32] thus sending us back to the *Histoire* to look beneath its apparently untroubled surface. Nancy Miller invites this kind of reading of Sand's novels, seeing them as a subtext to her autobiography, to be read alongside it as a way of filling in the gaps,[33] but perhaps the *Histoire* too, beneath its adoption of conventional modes of writing, reveals uncertainties and contradictions that are not so easily resolved. As Sand's daughter said: 'Celui qui débrouillera ma mère, celui-là sera bien malin.'[34]

Notes to Introduction

1. Baudelaire, *Œuvres complètes* (Paris: Gallimard, Pléiade, 1976), ii. 686–7.
2. Alfred de Vigny, *Œuvres complètes* (Paris: Gallimard, Pléiade, 1948), ii. 947.
3. Balzac, *Lettres à Madame Hanska* (Paris: Robert Laffont, 1990), i. 441.
4. Flaubert, *Correspondance*, ed. Descharmes (Paris: Librairie de France, 1924), iii. 645.
5. George Sand, *Correspondance*, ed. Georges Lubin (Paris: Garnier, 1985), ii. 880.
6. Sand, *Correspondance*, xx. 297.
7. See Isabelle Naginski, *George Sand, Writing for her Life* (New Brunswick: Rutgers University Press, 1991), 16–34, for a thorough discussion of Sand's androgyny.
8. See Bibliography for a list of the main works of autobiographical theory.
9. Paul de Man, 'Autobiography as de-facement', *Modern Language Notes* 94/2 (1979), 921.
10. See Bibliography for a list of recent studies of women's autobiography.

11. Quoted by Philippe Lejeune, *L'Autobiographie en France* (Paris: Armand Colin, 1971), 28.
12. Pierre Salomon, *George Sand, biographie* (Meylan: Editions de l'Aurore, 1984), 113.
13. Henry James, *French Poets and Novelists* (London: Macmillan, 1884), 155.
14. James: *French Poets and Novelists*, 154.
15. James, *French Poets and Novelists*, 156.
16. Helene Deutsch, *The Psychology of Women: a Psychoanalytic Interpretation* (London: Research Books Ltd, 1946).
17. See articles by Gita May and Marilyn Yalom, for example, in *The World of George Sand*, ed. Nathalie Datlof, Jeanne Fuchs and David A. Powell (Westport: Greenwood Press, 1991).
18. Nancy K. Miller, 'Women's autobiography in France', in *Women and Language in Literature and Society*, ed. Sally McConnell Ginet, Ruth Borker and Nelly Furman (Westport: Praeger Publishers, 1980).
19. Roy Pascal, *Design and Truth in Autobiography* (London: Routledge and Kegan Paul, 1960), 50.
20. Madame Roland, *Mémoires* (Paris: Mercure de France, 1966), 304.
21. To quote E. M. Sartori and D. W. Zimmerman (eds.), *French Women Writers, a Bio-bibliographical Source Book* (Westport: Greenwood Press, 1991), p. xxi: 'They could not engage in a professional activity without their husband's consent, nor could married women manage their property or any income they might earn.'
22. Sartori and Zimmerman (eds.), *French Women Writers*, 4.
23. George Sand, *Œuvres autobiographiques*, ed. Georges Lubin, 2 vols. (Paris: Gallimard, Pléiade, 1970–1).
24. For a complete collection of Sand's autobiographical writings, see *Œuvres autobiographiques* (n. 23 above).
25. See Marie Jacques Hoog, 'Lettres d'un voyageur: texte initiatique', *Colloque de Cérisy*, ed. Simone Vierne (Paris: Sedes, 1983).
26. Kathryn J. Crecelius, *Family Romances: George Sand's Early Novels* (Bloomington: Indiana University Press, 1987).
27. Tatiana Greene, 'De J. Sand à George Sand: Rose et Blanche de Sand et Sandeau et leur descendance', *Nineteenth-Century French Studies* (Spring 1976), 169–82.
28. Naomi Schor, *George Sand and Idealism* (Ithaca: Columbia University Press, 1993).
29. Thelma Jurgrau, 'Autobiography in general and George Sand's in particular', *Nineteenth-Century French Studies* (Fall 1988), 205. But see some revision of this view in her introduction to *George Sand, Story of my Life*, a group translation, ed. Thelma Jurgrau (State University of New York Press, 1991).
30. Sandra Gilbert and Susan Gubar, *The Madwoman in the Attic: The Woman Writer and the Nineteenth-Century Literary Imagination* (New Haven: Yale University Press, 1979), 73.
31. Gilbert and Gubar, *The Madwoman in the Attic*, 66.
32. Gilbert and Gubar, *The Madwoman in the Attic*, 69.
33. Miller, 'Women's autobiography in France'.
34. Quoted by Salomon, *George Sand*, 227.

CHAPTER 1

Autobiographical Project

I

Philippe Lejeune has defined the genre of autobiography as a pact between writer and reader which assumes that author, narrator and protagonist are the same person, and that the story the text tells is true. He points out that most autobiographies include an explicit address to the reader where the autobiographer introduces himself and explains what he is going to do and why, as though he feels the need to make clear exactly what the reader may expect from the text he is reading. This usually appears as a kind of preface: 'S'interroger sur le sens, les moyens, la portée de son geste, tel est le premier acte de l'autobiographe',[1] but it can also interrupt the narrative at any point as the autobiographer turns back on himself to comment on his own project. This self-consciousness, this tendency towards self-reflection and self-justification is more obvious in autobiographies than in other kinds of writing, perhaps because an autobiography is by definition a problematic text: fact and fiction, immediate and constructed, a hybrid, often containing within itself different kinds of writing from different times: letters, diary entries, authentic historical documents.

In this 'preface' which explicitly sets up the conditions of the text, the autobiographer usually justifies his writing in two ways: by stressing the intrinsic interest of his own personality and/or by seeing himself as representative of his time. Either way, the aim is to enlighten and improve, and thus to avoid accusations of vanity or self-indulgent nostalgia. Rousseau is typical in this respect, emphasizing his uniqueness as a person and also the uniqueness of his project at the beginning of the *Confessions*—'Je forme une entreprise qui n'eut jamais d'exemple, et dont l'exécution n'aura point d'imitateur. Je veux montrer à mes semblables un homme dans toute la vérité de la nature; et cet homme, ce sera moi. Moi seul [...]. Je ne suis fait comme aucun de ceux que j'ai vus'—yet also suggesting that this self-portrait may act as a 'première pièce de comparaison pour l'étude des hommes'.[2] Stendhal, writing the story of his life (or that of Henri Brulard) sixty years later and ten years or so before Sand, appears exclusively interested in finding out who he is, for himself and perhaps for a hypothetical close friend living in 1880: 'Je vais avoir cinquante ans, il serait bien temps de me connaître. Qu'ai-je été, que suis-je, en vérité je serais bien embarrassé de le dire.'[3] Chateaubriand conceives of his autobiography in both these ways at different times, and his published *Mémoires d'outre-tombe* reflect the various stages of its conception. In 1832, he saw himself as typical of his time: 'Si j'étais destiné à vivre, je représenterais dans ma personne, représentée dans mes Mémoires l'épopée de mon temps',[4] but in the Avant-Propos of 1846, his project seems more private and personal: to give a multi-layered picture of his inner life through time, largely, he says, for his wife.

   Both Stendhal and Chateaubriand clearly have Rousseau in mind when introducing their autobiographies, but Sand refers to him most explicitly and at greatest length in the opening pages of *Histoire de ma vie*, perhaps suggesting a certain anxiety with regard to her illustrious forebear and a need to explain her project by reference to his. For, while recognizing his greatness, she openly sets her narrative against the *Confessions*, emphasizing particularly the contrasts between them. She plays down any suggestion of her uniqueness, of her difference from others, and makes much of her solidarity with her fellows, embedding her own story in the history of her time. This is the reason she gives for including so lengthy an account of her ancestors back to the fourth generation, and in particular for devoting almost a third of the text to quoting letters between her father, her grandmother and her mother written before she was born. She exploits the fact that her story encompasses the recent history of France from the point of view not only of the aristocracy through her grandmother (illegitimate grand-daughter of the king of Poland) who was imprisoned in the aftermath of the Revolution, and her father, an officer in the Napoleonic army, but also of the people through her mother, daughter of a birdseller on the quays of Paris. She is '*à cheval* pour ainsi dire sur deux classes' (I, 629), and thus uniquely representative. As a child she had seen Napoleon, experienced the war in Spain and witnessed the miserable retreat of the French army from Europe; as an adult, she lived through the political upheavals of the 1830s and 40s. She saw history as fundamentally important (as did the realist novelists of her time), since public events made people what they were. She believed in the fatality of circumstance and saw everybody, peasant as well as nobleman, as the product of their heredity, while also allowing for the modifying action of free will. For her, history had a meaning and was going somewhere, and this faith in human progress and perfectibility counteracts her fatalism, informing also her political views, her Utopian socialism: 'Aujourd'hui l'étude de l'histoire peut être la théorie du progrès; elle peut tracer une ligne grandiose à laquelle viennent se rattacher toutes les lignes jusqu'alors éparses et brisées' (I, 800).

In this way, she justifies and excuses the inevitable emphasis on her own person as she writes her autobiography: in describing her development, she is giving us a history of her time, as a lesson for everyone; she is doing her duty, reluctantly, she says. She would rather not have to talk about herself, seeing it as 'ce besoin puéril chez l'homme et dangereux [...] chez l'artiste' (I, 8). She will only describe her life, her sufferings, in so far as these may help other people whose experiences have been similar. She attacks what she sees as Rousseau's exhibitionism, his obsessive focus on his own inner life, also because it involves accusing others rather than speaking on their behalf. She wishes to help her readers in the living of their lives, not hurt them by casting blame. In this way she aligns herself, albeit implicitly, with the holy St Augustine rather than the worldly Jean-Jacques: 'Le récit des souffrances et des luttes de la vie de chaque homme est donc l'enseignement de tous [...]. C'est dans cette vue sublime [...] que saint Augustin écrivit ses *Confessions*' (I, 10).

Although Sand never links her difference from Rousseau to her gender, this insistence in the opening pages of the *Histoire* on her typicality and therefore on her ordinariness, and the self-deprecatory tone which goes with it, are often thought to be characteristic of autobiographies by women, conditioned to see themselves as inferior to men, and as educators and carers rather than achievers:[5] 'J'éprouvais, je l'avoue, un dégoût mortel à occuper le public de ma personnalité, qui n'a rien de saillant, lorsque je me sentais le cœur et la tête remplis de personnalités plus fortes, plus logiques, plus complètes, plus idéales, de types supérieurs à moi-même' (I, 6). Sand seems here to be deliberately playing down what was exceptional about her person and her life in order to conform to conventional notions of what was womanly, to get her (male?) readers on her side. Do we not sense, however, a certain falseness in her modesty, since her story was undoubtedly an extraordinary one as she well knew? Indeed

it could be argued that this very emphasis on her mediocrity, her lack
of vanity, the parallel with St Augustine itself (as against Rousseau
with his unfortunate lapses in taste) acts as a kind of covert self-
idealizing more insidious and so arguably more effective than
Rousseau's blatant self-display. The one trivial misdeed which she
quotes as an example of her fallibility, her theft of money from her
grandmother's purse to give to the poor, is surely chosen because it is
so easily converted into a virtue. Thus her self-deprecation is distinctly
ambiguous. On the one hand, we are inclined to believe her when she
minimizes the importance of her work in the *Histoire*, declaring that
she forgets a book as soon as she has written it, particularly as this
casualness is confirmed by a later letter to her close friend, Flaubert:
'Je n'ai pas monté aussi haut que toi dans mon ambition. Tu veux
écrire pour les temps. Moi je crois que dans cinquante ans je serai
parfaitement oubliée et peut-être durement méconnue. C'est la loi des
choses qui ne sont pas de premier ordre et je ne me suis jamais crue
de 1er ordre.'[6] Elsewhere she ridicules the 'femme de lettres' that she
was, 'l'animal le moins intéressant et le plus mal peigné qui soit au
monde',[7] and contemporaries often commented on her unassuming
manner in company[8] and her generosity to others. On the other
hand, the very writing of one's autobiography, particularly in the
authoritative moralist's and historian's voice that she adopts, presupposes a certain self-confidence, the assumption that one's life story
is significant and worth telling, and the self that lived it worth
attending to. Perhaps there is no way out; perhaps true modesty and
the autobiographical project are incompatible, or perhaps Sand is
genuinely both diffident and arrogant at the same time, both 'female'
and 'male'.[9]

   The autobiographical pact, this explicit preface to the text, often
includes an undertaking to tell the truth, although not necessarily the
whole truth, and not always the truth in strict chronological order.
Unlike Rousseau, Sand makes it clear in the first paragraph of the
Histoire that she is going to be selective in the telling of her story,
including only those memories 'qui nous paraissent valoir la peine
d'être conservés' (I, 5), those that may act as 'un stimulant, un
encouragement, et même un conseil et un guide pour les autres esprits
engagés dans le labyrinthe de la vie' (I, 9), thus linking her selectivity
to her typicality as she sees it and to the overridingly moral aim of the
work. What then is the moral message of the *Histoire de ma vie* which
Sand saw as so important? What are the criteria which govern her

choice of material and in which direction does she wish to guide her readers?

One might expect her to be addressing herself, however covertly, to other women, to be speaking of her sufferings as especially representative of theirs, to be offering herself as she seems to offer Edmée and Consuelo among others as an example of how women should behave, and thus encourage other women to do as she did, take control of their own lives at whatever cost. Daniel Stern, although she follows Sand's example by adopting a male pseudonym, openly justifies her autobiography in this way, presenting it as the story by and of a successful woman written as an example for other women: 'Elle trouvait dans mon sexe même une raison décisive de parler [...]. Lorsqu'une femme s'est fait à elle-même sa vie, pensais-je alors, et que cette vie ne s'est pas gouvernée suivant la règle commune, elle en devient responsable, plus responsable qu'un homme, aux yeux de tous. Quand cette femme, par l'effet du hasard ou de quelque talent, est sortie de l'obscurité, elle a contracté, du même instant, des devoirs virils.'[10] Sand is never as clear as this. Just as we have seen the perspective of the *Histoire* to be double and contradictory, both female and male, so her explicit attitude to her own sex is distinctly ambiguous. She very rarely discusses her gender identification, as though she did not see it as a problem, and when she does, she seems rather uncomfortably to be having it both ways. Of course she is a woman, she says, nervous and emotional as all women are, and yet because of her education she thinks like a man and prefers the company of men. She accepts that the two sexes are different, implying through the vocabulary she chooses the inferiority of women (although she denies this), but she largely exempts herself from that difference: 'Je n'étais donc pas tout à fait une femme comme celles que censurent et raillent les moralistes' (II, 126–7). It is as though when writing in her own voice she has gone sufficiently beyond her own sex almost to cease to be aware of it, and perhaps this is why she does not use her autobiography in the way she uses some of her other works, explicitly as an example of their emancipation. Not seeing herself as a woman, she is not writing expressly for other women; the lesson she offers is universal, addressed to everybody. She preaches a vague kind of altruism, stressing the importance of love, the redemptive power of suffering; and any social awareness she demonstrates is of class rather than gender.[11] The implicit message of the *Histoire de ma vie*, however, its very denial of its own power as a story for women, is perhaps more challenging than an overt call to action would be. In the end it is up to the reader to extrapolate a feminist lesson from Sand's autobiography if she so wishes; she has not directly put it there.[12]

There is one area, however, in which Sand's feminism is clear, one issue on which she declares herself openly and unambiguously as a woman speaking for her sex, when she interrupts the story of her legal separation from her husband to give a generalized attack on the inequality and injustice of woman's position in marriage at that time. At the beginning of the *Histoire*, she says she will deal once and for all with the question of her marriage to Casimir, and here she refuses to cast any blame, in keeping with the discretion of her general approach which she maintains distinguishes her from Rousseau. But when she reaches this point in the narrative of her life, she is unable to sustain her tolerant, neutral tone as she attacks society's double standards, its assumption that a man is always master, and the text becomes pure polemic:

Mais ceci n'est rien encore, et l'homme est investi de bien d'autres droits. Il peut déshonorer sa femme, la *faire mettre en prison* et la condamner ensuite à rentrer sous sa dépendance, à subir son pardon et ses caresses! S'il lui épargne ce dernier outrage, le pire de tous, il peut lui faire une vie de fiel et d'amertume, lui reprocher sa faute à toutes les heures de sa vie, la tenir éternellement sous l'humiliation de la servitude, sous la terreur des menaces. (II, 380)

Although her husband did not stop her leading the life she had chosen in Paris, his presence as master of Nohant constantly marginalized her, put her in her place, and it was only when the separation was decided and Nohant was hers again that she could feel complete, take over his role as well as her own, be, as she puts it, 'à la fois père et mère de famille' (II, 406).

In spite of the sense of moral responsibility to others which prescribes what she will include and what she will omit fom her narrative, Sand also insists that she is telling the truth: 'je veux *taire* et non *arranger* ni *déguiser* plusieurs circonstances de ma vie' (II, 110). In order to arrive at this truth, all autobiographers rely heavily on memory: at one point in the *Histoire*, Sand celebrates one affective memory in particular: 'par un lien de souvenirs et de sensations que tout le monde connaît, sans pouvoir l'expliquer, je ne respire jamais des fleurs de liseron-vrille sans voir l'endroit des montagnes espagnoles

et le bord du chemin où j'en cueillis pour la première fois' (I, 557).
We shall see later how certain other incidents of her childhood, those
associated with excessive pain or pleasure, seem still to live on in her
almost in spite of herself and are described with an exceptional
vividness which we may take as a measure of their authenticity. But
memories, involuntary or voluntary, are necessarily selective. By them
the past is changed as the autobiographer, whether consciously or
not, filters out the unacceptable and highlights the retrospectively
significant; thus any claim to truthfulness is not necessarily being
made in bad faith. Although in Sand's case it is difficult not to accuse
her of deliberate deception when she doctors her father's letters to her
mother and grandmother in order to project a more romantic picture
of his love for them both, elsewhere the misrepresentations and
suppressions for which she is blamed are less conscious and, as we shall
see, revealing in themselves.

   Her own view of her autobiography once she had finished it is
interestingly contradictory. In 1851 she wrote in a letter to Pierre
Bocage: 'Achetez donc mes mémoires à mon éditeur. Cela, c'est une
bonne chose, je vous assure, et je ne ferai jamais mieux.'[13] But in 1868
she is less sure of herself: 'Je m'imaginais me résumer, est-ce qu'on
peut se résumer? Est-ce qu'on peut se connaître? Est-ce qu'on est
jamais QUELQU'UN? Je n'en sais plus rien. Il me semble qu'on
change de jour en jour et qu'au bout de quelques années, on est un
être nouveau' (II, 630), although it could be that this uncertainty
refers only to fragmented diary entries later published as *Sketches* and
Hints. Ultimately, perhaps the double perspective given in a retrospective autobiography comes nearer to expressing the complexities
and obscurities of the 'real' person, provided we are alert to how we
read.

2

An autobiographer's explicit statements about his text, whether inside
or outside it, must always be complemented by the implicit message
which emerges from the way he has chosen to depict himself. 'Que la
trompette du jugement dernier sonne quand elle voudra; je viendrai,
ce livre à la main, me présenter devant le souverain juge. Je dirai
hautement: voilà ce que j'ai fait, ce que j'ai pensé, ce que je fus.'[14]
Rousseau is not the only one to have written the story of his life
partly as a defence of who he was and what he did, although most

state it less clearly and certainly less dramatically than he did. This has long been recognized as one of the (possibly unconscious) motivations behind an autobiographical text which colours the picture the author gives of himself, although as in Rousseau's and indeed Gide's case there is often a confusion between the confession of guilt and an affirmation of innocence. The reader needs to approach an auto- biography in much the same way as he does a novel, critically, conscious of the subterfuges of language and form, in order to reach what Roy Pascal calls 'the cone of darkness at the centre'.[15]

It has perhaps been even more difficult for women to tell the whole truth about themselves since those ideal qualities which culturally have been associated with womanhood, selflessness and modesty, are incompatible with the sense of one's uniqueness implicit in the autobiographical project itself—as has already been suggested. Women have used different strategies to evade this contradiction: some tell their own story by telling the story of someone else, husband, friend, the community in which they live, as though they can only find themselves by identification with another.[16] Others censor their lives, presenting only the public, acceptable face, playing down the shocking or traumatic, producing what Sidonie Smith, speaking of Harriet Martineau's autobiography, calls the public version of her life, 'the most carefully controlled, the most rational, authoritative, legitimate. They are, that is, the most "masculine".'[17] Either way, the story of her own emancipation which is usually implicit in an autobiography by a woman has had its sting removed, in the second case by denying the cost of the emancipation and in the first by concealing that it is a woman's story at all.

Sand too plays down the more disquieting implications of her life, clearly anxious not to shock or alienate her readership. But this 'sanitization', as it has been called,[18] could be explained as much by her theory of aesthetic idealism with its roots in her Utopian socialism as by her fear of offending. She states quite clearly, in the preface to *La Mare au diable*, for example, and also in the *Histoire de ma vie* (II, 161), that art should elevate and idealize, not depress and discourage. She sees no point in depicting the evil or the ugly: she will fulfil her role as educator by inspiring her reader with admirable examples, not by reminding him of the base reality he knows already: 'J'ai excusé les fautes, j'ai grandi les caractères, j'ai *tu* les misères réelles. C'est comme cela qu'il faut écrire certaines histoires et c'est comme cela que, par égard pour tant d'autres, j'ai écrit, mon cher Buloz, *L'histoire de ma vie.*[19] For Sand, the process of literary creation went necessarily and unashamedly with one of idealization. Thus she refashions her story and that of others not so much because she is a woman as because she is a certain kind of writer, although Lanson talks of her 'optimisme féminin'[20] as though she was that kind of writer precisely because she was a woman; and Naomi Schor too, while highlighting her idealism as her main characteristic, sees it as her way of being a woman in a man's world, 'a strategy for bodying forth her difference'.[21]

Sand begins the *Histoire* not with her own life but with that of her parents, and by altering her father's letters to his wife, she deliberately transforms their story into an exemplary romance between a generous and passionate young aristocrat and a pure-hearted working girl. She makes little of their less than chaste past, of the illegitimate children they had both already borne, passing rapidly over her mother's experience as a kept woman and shifting the emphasis in her father's case away from his seduction of a local peasant girl onto her grandmother's saintliness in taking charge of his natural son, who was to be Sand's companion throughout her childhood at Nohant. She compares their story to a novel—'La vie de cet homme fut un roman de guerre et d'amour' (I, 77)—openly dramatizes their first meeting and emphasizes their loyalty and love for each other during their forbidden rendez-vous at La Châtre and later after their secret marriage.

When Sand eventually embarks on her presentation of herself, the process of 'sanitization' continues. Since she sees her autobiography as fact rather than fiction at least where she herself is concerned, she insists that she will do nothing to deny her own complexity: 'j'étais d'une étoffe trop bigarrée pour me prêter à une idéalisation quelconque' (II, 160), and it is true that she makes much of her double, contradictory nature, melancholy and gay, introspective and sociable, world-weary and childlike all at the same time.[22] But we still feel that the sharp edges have been blunted and the most controversial aspects of her life and personality denied. For example, she says almost nothing of her love affairs and their associated pain which comes out clearly in her letters and in the *Journal intime* of 1834. She displaces her infatuation with Aurélien de Sèze into descriptions of her exhilaration as she rode on horseback through the Pyrenean landscape, taken from the diary she kept at the time before the friendship had really begun. She omits completely any reference to her passion for Musset, does not mention the doctor, Pagello, with whom she also had an affair in

Venice,[23] indeed gives the briefest of accounts of her traumatic, ill-fated stay in that city, concentrating on the practical difficulties the couple encountered and the popular charm of the Venetian theatre. She does describe her relationship with Chopin but domesticates it, stressing her maternal care of him and playing down any sexual intimacy; indeed the fact that this is probably a fair picture may explain her willingness to dwell at more length on their time together. Her undoubtedly passionate affair with Michel de Bourges becomes largely a fraternal friendship based on her new-found fascination with his socialist ideas, and on their intellectual exchange of views.

Indeed, throughout the *Histoire*, as a way of denying her sexuality, she stresses the importance of male friendship rather than love, privileging this chaste comradeship as the most precious of bonds. She quotes Montaigne in her support while refusing to agree that she is incapable of such a bond because she is a woman: 'Avec lui [François Rollinat] et pour lui, je fis le code de la véritable et saine amitié, d'une amitié à la Montaigne, toute de choix, d'élection et de perfection' (II, 129). She insists on describing her young *berrichon* companions as though they were brothers (which Jules Sandeau, at least, most definitely was not). Almost all the friends of whom she gives portraits towards the end of the *Histoire* are male—Delacroix, Sainte-Beuve, Calamatta, Gustave Planche, Charles Didier—and she clearly ungenders the friendship by concentrating more on their ideas than on their personalities or their lives. She hardly mentions her (few) women friends: Marie d'Agoult, for example, with whom she travelled in Switzerland and who stayed at Nohant as a guest, is only referred to briefly in passing and then rather coolly, perhaps because she became as much rival as friend. It is as though Sand wishes to present herself as beyond her sex, an honorary man.

The one exception to this is Marie Dorval, and the first few pages of the chapter devoted to her are significantly confused. It is here that Sand states most categorically that she prefers the company of men— 'A très peu d'exceptions près, je ne supporte pas longtemps la société des femmes' (II, 223)—at the same time describing Marie as 'le résumé de l'inquiétude féminine arrivée à sa plus haute puissance' (II, 224), that is, all that Sand most despises in her own sex. Yet she proceeds to tell Marie's story in detail and with an emotional sympathy quite absent from the portraits of her male friends, suggestive of a close identification with this artist woman defeated and destroyed by the

conflicting demands made upon her. Thelma Jurgrau suggests convincingly that Sand saw a resemblance between Marie and her own
mother,[24] but the resemblance is also perhaps closer to home. She makes
much of Marie's maternity, the conflict between her love for her children
and the need to work for the money with which to bring them up. She
describes her difficult relationship with her daughter, who rashly entered
into an unsuitable marriage and then made heavy financial demands.
She quotes the letters Marie wrote on the death of her grandson, and
her son-in-law's letters to her on Marie's own death. The chapter ends
with a passionate declaration of love and grief (which partly supports
those who see their friendship as a Lesbian affair):

Oui, si elle a été trahie et souillée, cette victime de l'art et de la destinée, elle
a été aussi bien chérie et bien regrettée. Et je n'ai pas parlé de moi, de moi
qui ne me suis pas encore habituée à l'idée qu'elle n'est plus, et que je ne
pourrai plus la secourir et la consoler; de moi, qui n'ai pu raconter cette
histoire et transcrire ces détails sans me sentir étouffée par les larmes; de moi,
qui ai la conviction de la retrouver dans un meilleur monde. (II, 248–9)

Much of what Sand says of Marie also applied to her: she too was torn
between her professional life and her children, suffered from the
jealousy and irrational behaviour of her daughter Solange, and was
vilified by some of her contemporaries. So perhaps in this chapter of
the *Histoire* she is telling the private story of her woman friend because
she could not truly tell her own without compromising the gender-
free image she wished to project. In the same way, when describing
her father's family at the very beginning of the autobiography, Sand
picks out Madame Dupin de Chenonceaux who was her great-
grandfather's second wife, and so in no way related to her, but to
whom she was drawn for her goodness and intelligence. Once again,
embedded in a story about men (she was also a friend of Rousseau
and the *philosophes*), this figure of an exemplary woman shines out
briefly as an ideal of femininity which Sand would not or could not
present directly.

When talking about herself she tends to play down her own gender.
For example, she denies again and again that she was in any way
sexually alluring, purposely discounting the attraction of the unusual.
She concedes when she first introduces herself that her readers will
expect a physical description and mockingly provides a passport
portrait: 'yeux noirs, cheveux noirs, front ordinaire, teint pâle, nez
bien fait, menton rond, bouche moyenne, taille quatre pieds dix

pouces, signes particuliers, aucun' (I, 467–8). Compare this with
Daniel Stern's detailing of her stereotypical blond good looks in *Mes
Souvenirs*,[25] or Madame Roland's emphasis in her *Mémoires* on her
dark-haired beauty.[26] In this way, Sand both invites us to see her as a
person not a woman (her description could equally well be that of a
man, apart from the height), and also wittily makes us aware how far
a woman's identity is conventionally associated with her body, how
unexpected it is for her to position herself as anonymous, unfixed
subject rather than fixed object of desire. She presents her plainness,
'ni laide ni belle' (I, 467), as a liberation: it meant she could disregard
her appearance and be herself. In fact, of course, at least at certain
periods of her life, she exploited her striking looks, dressed
flamboyantly, playing with different kinds of costume in an act of
display as well as disguise. This is what had made her notorious and
this is the side of herself she now wants to suppress. She equally plays
down her choice at certain times of male dress, stressing its practicality,
the anonymity it gave her, and quoting examples of other women
(including her mother) who had adopted it, thus detaching it from
any deliberate gender transgression.

Similarly she insists on her stupidity, her inability to think
effectively and consecutively, attributing this in part to her lack of a
formal education—'Mon esprit, à demi cultivé, était à certains égards
une table rase, à d'autres égards une sorte de chaos' (II, 273)—and also
to her temperament. She still is as she was then: 'je ne songeais à rien.
J'ai passé les trois quarts de ma vie ainsi, et pour ainsi dire à l'état
latent' (I, 937). She goes on, though, to link her vacant mind both to
her childish capacity to dream and so to her literary vocation, and also
to her goodness, thus cleverly turning it into a mark of her superiority
(as we saw her do earlier with her ordinariness). She has remained a
child all her life, she says, artless and innocent, easily amused but
equally easily victimized and imposed upon. She talks of her
'simplicité, résultat d'une plénitude de cœur' (II, 439), of her nature
which is 'confiante et tendre' (I, 780). Without openly accusing
others (unlike Rousseau, she says), she avoids all blame, in connection
with her estrangement from her aristocratic relatives for example, or
her separation from her husband. Any mistake she made was the result
of her devotion to others, since she had realized early on that she
could only be happy through love. Temperamentally as well as
philosophically an idealist, she always tried to think the best of other
people:

dans toutes les conditions où j'ai été libre de choisir ma manière d'être, j'ai cherché un moyen d'idéaliser la réalité autour de moi et de la transformer en une sorte d'oasis fictive, où les méchants et les oisifs ne seraient pas tentés d'entrer ou de rester. Un songe d'âge d'or, un mirage d'innocence champêtre, artiste ou poétique, m'a prise dès l'enfance et m'a suivie dans l'âge mûr. (II, 41)

Her lack of sophistication and her directness also brought her close to the people, and she always, she says, treated her servants and the peasants on her estate as equals. She hopes for a future 'quand le temps et le progrès auront fait justice de la race des laquais pour ne laisser autour de nous que des fonctionnaires, nos amis parfois, nos égaux toujours' (I, 769), thus aligning herself deliberately with her proletarian mother rather than her aristocratic grandmother. And yet there is no doubt that the homely, guileless persona that she projects, innocent and unthreatening, is largely at odds with her complex personality, with the facts of her controversial life and with the assured tone she adopts in her autobiography. She certainly commanded loyalty and devotion as the 'Bonne Dame de Nohant', for example, but equally she never lost her sense of her own position and would not have dreamt of selling Nohant and becoming truly one of the people.

One of the oddest features of Sand's autobiography is the way the first 500 pages are taken up by an account of her ancestors and particularly by the quotation of her father's letters to his mother and wife when he was away in Paris and in the army. This becomes a kind of biography in its own right and she calls it 'l'histoire de mon père' (I, 307) told in parallel with her own *Histoire*. She says that she vowed to write it at the age of 16 on the night just after her grandmother died, when her father's tomb was opened and, persuaded by her tutor, she kissed his skull in a final, macabre gesture of farewell, twelve years after his death. As well as parsimoniously exploiting the letters as extra copy, Sand here seems to be doing what many women autobiographers have done,[27] appending her story to that of a more prestigious male; elsewhere she describes her father as 'le véritable auteur de l'histoire de ma vie' (I, 156). This appears as yet another way of playing herself down, as though she can only possibly arouse interest as the offspring of her heroic and romantic father. Alternatively, she could be introducing her own life via the male heroics of war so as to benefit from a kind of reflected glory. Or perhaps it is not really the fighting she is interested in, but the idealized love between her father and grandmother, with which, as we shall see later, she identifies as both mother and son. Thus she may be indirectly writing about herself when writing about him. Whatever Sand's reasons, since the last section of the *Histoire* tails off into portraits of her friends who are almost all male, the framing of her narrative within those of men works to privilege male achievement as a necessary context for a woman's story rather than to highlight that story for itself.

Most women writers at least before the twentieth century were childless, and writing and motherhood are often seen as parallel but incompatible, the one conscious and intellectual, the other natural and physiological. As Margaret Homans puts it: 'Motherhood is literal creativity. It must be difficult for a woman to choose as her vocation poetry or figurative creativity, perhaps to the detriment of the maternal vocation with which she is expected to be contented, because the values associated with motherhood and with poetry are so very different.'[28] Sand is one of the few to have achieved both, being at the same time mother and writer although not a poet, apparently sacrificing nothing, fully a woman as well as vicariously male. Colette marvels at how she managed to do it all: 'Comment diable s'arrangeait George Sand?'[29] Sand's letters constantly demonstrate her loving concern for her children's well-being during and in spite of her numerous absences, her need for them and her delight when they were reunited, significantly comparing her son and herself to 'deux amants qui se retrouvent'.[30] Yet she only very occasionally allows this passion to emerge in her autobiography. During her account of her first pregnancy, she briefly expresses her solidarity with her own sex as she celebrates the womanly work of sewing the baby's layette, and the birth itself is presented as a moment of pure joy: 'Ce fut le plus beau moment de ma vie que celui où, après une heure de profond sommeil qui succéda aux douleurs terribles de cette crise, je vis en m'éveillant ce petit être endormi sur mon oreiller' (II, 37). But in the end, such 'conventionally female moments' (as Nancy Miller calls them)[31] turn out to be less of a climax and revelation than first appears. She makes little of her daily care of Maurice, and the birth of Solange is passed over very rapidly as the fact is announced bluntly with no warning or preparation and Sand confesses to a certain feeling of anti-climax: 'J'avais beaucoup désiré avoir une fille, et cependant je n'éprouvai pas la joie que Maurice m'avait donnée' (II, 90). From now on, the children are mentioned only briefly, usually in connection with her concern for their education, and the tone is reflective and dispassionate, her adoration of Maurice only surfacing, abruptly and shockingly, in one sudden reference to her pain on leaving him at school: 'Je crus que j'allais mourir' (II, 178). Sand's feeling for her young lovers was often maternal, and significantly it is when speaking of Chopin that she makes her most revealing statement on a mother's love: 'J'avais pour l'artiste une sorte d'adoration maternelle très vive, très vraie, mais qui ne pouvait pas un instant lutter contre l'amour des entrailles, le seul sentiment chaste qui puisse être passionné' (II, 433). She insisted on taking Solange to live with her in Paris in the early years of her separation from her husband, but in the *Histoire* she plays down both the strangeness and the practical difficulties of that decision. She refused in her life to allow her motherhood to constrain her freedom, and in her autobiography she largely omits both the joys and the pains which motherhood brings. These are specifically the emotions of a woman, and therefore at odds with the universal image Sand wished to project and the male tradition within which she was writing.

As both narrator and protagonist, then, through what she says explicitly in justification and explanation of her text, and through what is implied by her presentation of her younger self, Sand largely conforms to male expectations of what a (woman's) autobiography should be. She has not the arrogance to assume her story is interesting in itself. It will be read because it is representative of her time, because she was surrounded by exemplary men from whom she has acquired a certain worldly wisdom, because her femaleness is asexual and therefore does not threaten; and, as we saw earlier, perhaps she did regard herself in this way, as ungendered, androgynous. Yet this is not necessarily the whole picture; we are also conscious of another truth, for inevitably, at odd moments, in different ways, her essential womanhood does burst through—when pleading for a wife's equality with her husband in marriage, mourning the death of her woman friend, Marie Dorval, or remembering her desolation at being separated from her son—and such moments occur most frequently in those central sections of the *Histoire* which deal with her childhood, adolescence and early married life. Here we are necessarily concerned more specifically with a girl and young woman who had not yet found her adult identity and gone beyond her sex. We learn of her passionate attachment to her mother from whom she was separated, her education at home then in a convent, her early marriage to someone she hardly knew, the birth of her two children followed by a boredom and depression which she barely understood, and finally her liberation away from home as a professional writer. Only a woman could have lived and told this story, and it is in the telling of it, at the core of the text, that Sand is at her most vivid and unconsciously revealing.

Notes to Chapter 1

1. Lejeune, *L'Autobiographie en France*, 72.
2. Rousseau, *Confessions* (Paris: Gallimard, Pléiade, 1959), i. 5, 3.
3. Stendhal, *Vie de Henri Brulard*, *Œuvres intimes* (Paris: Gallimard, Pléiade, 1955), 38.
4. Chateaubriand, *Mémoires d'outre-tombe* (Paris: Gallimard, Pléiade, 1951), i. xiii.
5. This idea is expressed clearly, for example, in Patricia Meyer Spacks' chapter, 'Female rhetorics', in *The Private Self: Theory and Practice of Women's Autobiographical Writing*, ed. Shari Benstock (London: Routledge, 1988).
6. Sand, *Correspondance*, xxiii. 332.
7. Sand, *Correspondance*, ii. 292.
8. See Curtis Cate, *George Sand, A Biography* (New York: Avon Books, 1976), 625–6 and 687, for the reactions of Elizabeth Barrett Browning and the Goncourt brothers respectively.
9. See also Jane Marcus, 'Private selves of public women', in *The Private Self*, ed. Benstock, for elaboration of this paradox.
10. Daniel Stern, *Mes Souvenirs* (Paris: Calmann Lévy, 1880), pp. viii-ix.
11. See her appeal to peasants and artisans to write their own story and that of their ancestors (ii. 28).
12. See her refusal to stand for election to the French Academy and her opposition to women's suffrage. A convincing account of the extent of Sand's feminism is given in Donna Dickenson, *George Sand: a Brave Man, the Most Womanly Woman* (Oxford: Berg, 1988).
13. Sand, *Correspondance*, x. 483.
14. Rousseau, *Confessions*, i. 5.
15. Pascal, *Design and Truth in Autobiography*, 184.
16. See Mary G. Mason, 'The other voice: autobiographies of women writers', in *Autobiography: Essays Theoretical and Critical*, ed. James Olney (Princeton: Princeton University Press, 1980).
17. Sidonie Smith, *A Poetics of Women's Autobiography* (Bloomington: Indiana University Press, 1987), 148.
18. Michael Sheringham, *French Autobiography: Devices and Desires* (Oxford: Clarendon Press, 1993), 116.
19. Sand, *Correspondance*, xv. 344.
20. Gustave Lanson, *Histoire de la littérature française* (Paris: Hachette, 1951), 998.
21. Schor, *George Sand and Idealism*, 47.
22. See also Ch. 4.
23. See also the first three *Lettres d'un voyageur*.

24. Thelma Jurgrau, introduction to *George Sand, Story of my Life*.
25. Stern, *Mes Souvenirs*, 309.
26. Madame Roland, *Mémoires*, 254.
27. See n. 15 above.
28. Margaret Homans, *Women Writers and Poetic Identity* (Princeton: Princeton University Press, 1980), 223.
29. Colette, *L'Etoile Vesper (Souvenirs)* (Geneva: Editions du Milieu du Monde, 1946), 214.
30. Sand, *Correspondance*, ii. 132.
31. Miller, 'Women's autobiography in France', 263.

CHAPTER 2

Family Relationships

Since Rousseau, autobiographies have focused more on childhood as
the origin of and key to the adult; and a child's life is necessarily
dominated by the presence (or absence) of its parents. Richard Coe,
in his study of childhood narratives, notices the predominance of
unusual and unbalanced family relationships in the childhoods of
autobiographers. They may be characterized by a dominant parent
with the other weak, indifferent or absent,[1] or by a grandparent who
takes over a parent's role. The shape of the autobiographical narrative
is often determined by the pattern of the relationship between a
parent and the narrator whose conscious or unconscious aim in
writing his life story is to recover what he has lost or come to terms
with what he missed. This clearly takes us back to Freud's
narrativizing into different, possibly traumatic, stages of the child's
relationship with his mother and father. Autobiographers can be seen
as their own psychoanalysts, 'making what is in itself unpleasurable
into a subject to be recollected and worked over in the mind'.[2]

Freud notoriously has difficulty tracing the development of the
little girl into and through the Oedipal stage; he makes less of it,
contradicts himself and is considerably less convincing. In broad
terms, he stresses the growing ambivalence of the little girl's
relationship with her mother in the pre-Oedipal stage, which will
eventually lead her to shift the object of her desire from her mother
to her father and so into heterosexuality. This ambivalence he attributes in part to her castration complex, her discovery of her own lack
(of a penis) for which she blames her mother. Before this, in the so-
called phallic phase, Freud suggests, she had been just like her brother:
'We are now obliged to recognize that the little girl is a little man.'[3]
All small children are bisexual; it is relatively straightforward for the
little boy to move out of the pre-Oedipal stage into an Oedipal
attachment to his mother and so into heterosexuality since the gender

of his love object does not change, but for Freud 'the development of a little girl into a normal woman is more difficult and more complicated'.[4] She keeps her relationship with her mother but it needs to be revised and renegotiated. Thus, in order to prefer her father, she has to see her mother and therefore herself as inferior (because lacking a penis); her attachment to her mother, from being largely positive in its pre-Oedipal phase, becomes more negative while remaining intense. This theory which defines woman against a male norm suggests the difficulty a woman will have in acquiring a strong, confident sense of her own identity as female.

Recent commentators, led by Nancy Chodorow, while not denying the importance of the pre-Oedipal phase for little boys, stress the special strength and permanence of the bond with the mother for little girls, its positive, nurturing qualities as well as the need to outgrow it. Both aspects contribute crucially to a woman's acquisition of a sense of herself with, as well as against, her mother, female like herself, by identification as well as separation: 'A girl tends to retain elements of her preoedipal primary love and primary identification [...]. The ease of this identification and the feeling of continuity with her mother conflict with a girl's felt need to separate from her.'[5] This revision of Freud revalorizes the feminine as both mother and daughter and puts this relationship, rather than that with the father, at the centre of the little girl's development. As Virginia Woolf famously said, 'we think back through our mothers if we are women',[6] and the triad of grandmother, mother, daughter can be seen as an alternative to the more usual family triangle of father, mother, child.

It is unsurprising then that mothers (and often grandmothers) are central to women's autobiographies, whether the daughter is celebrating her mother's all-encompassing and liberating presence, as Colette does, rebelling against her restrictive conventionality, like Simone de Beauvoir, or stressing the doubleness and ambivalence of this primary bond, as we see in some of Marguerite Duras's autobiographical writings. There is a peculiar intensity in the way a woman writer talks about her mother since it is largely to her that she owes that sense of self which gives her the confidence to write her own life story. Her mother is bound to act as a kind of role model, transmitting positive or negative values within and against which her daughter finds herself; and she can be seen to address her autobiography in part to her, either to repay a debt of gratitude or finally to get her own back (or both). As Bella Brodski says (of

Nathalie Sarraute's *Enfance* and Christa Wolf's *Patterns of Childhood*), 'these autobiographical narratives are generated out of a compelling need to enter into discourse with the absent or distant mother'.[7]

Sand's life and the way she tells it in her autobiography demonstrate particularly clearly the relevance of such perspectives, and the most fruitful readings of the *Histoire de ma vie* have been those influenced by psychoanalytic theory. She spent the first years of her life in a small Paris flat in an idyllically close intimacy with her mother (and her half-sister who acted as a kind of second mother). Her father was away fighting in the Napoleonic wars, appearing only intermittently as a benign and loving presence. The family briefly followed him to Madrid in 1808 where they lived for a few months before the fortunes of war turned and they were forced to leave. They took refuge in Nohant, the country property in the Berry, bought by Sand's widowed paternal grandmother just after the Revolution. A few weeks later her father was suddenly killed in a riding accident when little Aurore was 4. From then on she was brought up in Nohant by and between her mother and grandmother who fought bitterly for the child's loyalty and love. Both were mourning Aurore's father and looked to her to make up for his loss. Sand repeatedly insists in her *Histoire* on the distress her role as bone of contention caused her, also linking her later political views to her early experiences as victim: 'Mon pauvre cœur d'enfant commençait à être ballotté par leur rivalité. Objet d'une jalousie et d'une lutte perpétuelles, il était impossible que je ne fusse pas la proie de quelque prévention, comme j'étais la victime des douleurs que je causais' (I, 658), and again: 'Pour ne parler que du commencement de ma vie, ma mère et ma grand-mère, avides de mon affection, s'arrachèrent les lambeaux de mon cœur' (I, 682–3).

This conflict is polarized by Sand so that her two mothers, as she calls them, appear as fundamentally opposing types, reflecting to some extent the conventional stereotypes of angel and monster,[8] although clearly and interestingly (as we shall see later) Sand reverses the value attached to each. Her grandmother is rational, controlled, ultra-civilized; her mother passionate, hot-tempered, almost primitive:

C'étaient vraiment les deux types extrêmes de notre sexe: l'une blanche, blonde, grave, calme et digne dans ses manières, une véritable Saxonne de noble race, aux grands airs pleins d'aisance et de bonté protectrice; l'autre brune, pâle, ardente, gauche et timide devant les gens du beau monde, mais toujours prête à éclater quand l'orage grondait trop fort au-dedans, une nature d'Espagnole, jalouse, passionnée, colère et faible, méchante et bonne en même temps. (I, 605–6)

As the last phrase suggests, her mother is herself seen as double, both good and bad, tenderly loving and unjustly angry in turn. This polarization reappears in the description of the child's terrifying dream in which the two female figures in the pattern of the wallpaper of her bedroom come to life. The one, seen as aggressive bacchante, advances on and attacks the other, presented as a timid nymph. Lucienne Frappier-Mazur sees the recurrence of doubles in the *Histoire*, the splitting off of good from bad, as the child's way of dealing with her difficult, ambivalent relationship with her mother, which allowed her to love the good in her and reject the bad.[9] Characters in Sand's novels also often appear in pairs, Rose and Blanche, Indiana and Noun, Lélia and Pulchérie, Consuelo and Corilla, partly of course as literary stereotypes since this is a fundamental way of structuring human nature (and there are also male doubles, the twins in *La Petite Fadette* for example), but corresponding perhaps also to her mother's double-sided nature, the dual influences of mother and grandmother (reflected also in the opposing characters of their two personal maids), and her own resulting alternative identities. Doubleness appears as a basic structure of Sand's thinking undoubtedly in part as a result of her crucial childhood years.

The central opposition as presented in the autobiography is clearly between mother and grandmother rather than within either, and their temperamental difference is exacerbated by the difference in social class, each one's lack of understanding of the values and ways of thinking of the other leading to a hostility which traumatized the young Aurore. It was inevitable that the older Madame Dupin, mistress of Nohant, would win against her penniless daughter-in-law and a financial arrangement was eventually concluded whereby Aurore's mother was in effect bought off, being promised a regular income if she left her daughter to the care of her grandmother in Nohant and went to live in Paris, returning only for occasional holidays in the summer. Thus Aurore was repeatedly abandoned, the separations from her mother becoming longer and longer until she finally accepted that her mother no longer really loved her. She spent the years between 14 and 16 in a convent in Paris, in a community of English Augustinian nuns, her grandmother seeing this as a remedy for the bad behaviour her unhappiness had caused in her, and a year and a half after she returned to Nohant her grandmother, now her substitute mother, died. A childhood and adolescence thus characterized by contrast, conflict and abandonment may well account for the difficulty Aurore had in developing a 'normal' relationship to her own gender, and give credence to the various psychoanalytical interpretations of her life and autobiography.

In order to explain Sand's contradictory gender identifications and their resolution into a kind of androgyny, these readings tend to privilege either her absent father or her unsatisfied love for her mother, although still taking account of both. Helene Deutsch, writing in 1945 in the wake of Freud, gives Sand as a clear example of a 'masculinity complex' which was 'a consequence of her thwarted thrust towards femininity'.[10] She shows how difficult it was for the young Aurore to identify with her mother in the normal way since her love for her was constantly put under strain, either through her grandmother's hostility which also antagonized the child, or through her mother's own abandonment of her. At the same time, she was led to identify with her dead father both indirectly through her passion for her mother and directly by her grandmother who repeatedly saw her father in her: 'Ma voix, mes traits, mes manières, mes goûts, tout en moi lui rappelait son fils enfant, à tel point qu'elle se faisait quelquefois, en me regardant jouer, une sorte d'illusion, et que souvent elle m'appelait Maurice et disait *mon fils* en parlant de moi' (I, 603).

Indeed there is a further parallel between Aurore and her father, torn as they both were between the same two women. Sand's extensive quoting and altering in the *Histoire* of her father's letters expressing his passionate love for both his mother and his wife suggest clearly the different ways in which she saw herself as him. Thus she idealizes the love between him and his mother perhaps as a substitute for something she never had and always yearned for (although there is a reference here too to the loving intimacy between her son, also Maurice, and herself): 'Il aime sa mère comme la fille ne l'aime point [a comparison here with Sand's daughter, Solange] et ne pourra jamais l'aimer. Noyé dans le bonheur d'être chéri sans partage et choyé avec adoration, cette mère est pour lui l'objet d'une sorte de culte' (I, 76). Or she brings out his femininity, paradoxically in the same passage: 'Il était beau comme une fleur, chaste et doux comme une jeune fille' (I, 76), later stressing directly her own resemblance to him: 'Mon être est un reflet, affaibli sans doute, mais assez complet, du sien [...]. Ma vie extérieure a autant différé de la sienne que l'époque où elle s'est développée; mais eussé-je été garçon et eussé-je vécu vingt-cinq ans plus tôt, je sais et je sens que j'eusse agi et senti en toutes choses comme mon père' (I, 156–7). The strength of this identification, together with her unsatisfactory relationship with both her mother and grandmother, suggests according to Deutsch that Sand was unable properly to be a woman, to develop naturally from a close pre-Oedipal attachment to her mother to desire for a real father who is different from herself, and thence into heterosexual love. Deutsch sees her either as distorting her feminine sexuality into the maternal but used cruelly and aggressively as she felt she was used by her mother, or as choosing to be a man; either way femininity is discredited in favour of the male.

Kathryn Crecelius and Naomi Schor agree with Deutsch in stressing the importance of the absent father in Sand's self-construction, supporting this view through a more sophisticated reading of the *Histoire* (as well as of Sand's other works). Both make much of the centrality of the father in the first part of the text and of Sand's insistence on her aristocratic paternal inheritance. Unlike Deutsch, though, they present Sand's life story as a triumph, ascribed by Crecelius to 'the lack of paternal constraint in Aurore Dupin's life along with her positive image of her father',[11] both only possible because he is dead. His absence is thus seen as an advantage, allowing her to become 'a woman writing, living independently, practicing a profession like a man, while not surrendering her female side'.[12] Crecelius sees the *Histoire* as having been written to and for him, as a debt of gratitude, as opposed to the *Voyage en Auvergne*, which she began for her mother and was unable to continue. Schor agrees: 'Much of Sand's oeuvre can be seen as driven by a constant struggle to overcome the pull of the discredited maternal idealization, in favor of the more prestigious paternal.'[13] The autobiography with its privileging of the father[14] represents one stage in the process of 'her truly astonishing transformation of herself from an object of scandal into the supreme figure of propriety, the good mother par excellence, the popular public persona and cultural artifact that came to be known as the "Bonne Dame de Nohant"'.[15]

An alternative view of this process places Sand's intense relationship with her mother firmly at the centre, thus going against the grain of conventional nineteenth-century narratives in which the exclusively

feminine mother–daughter bond is usually subordinate.[16] It is easy to
see Sand's story as dominated by a matriarchal line symbolized by the
ring which her grandmother gave her to give her mother on her first
meeting with her as a baby, and which Sand says she now still wears,
a line which she herself carried on when she left her husband and
took over his role. The handing down of the maternal identity was,
however, fraught with difficulty. Bozon-Scalzetti goes back to Helene
Deutsch in interpreting Sand's attachment to her mother as disappointed homosexual desire but makes it all-important, using it
exclusively to explain Sand's masculinization;[17] it becomes the subtext
to both her life and her writing, and her autobiography is seen as a
desperate letter to her mother written through and in parallel to her
father's letters to his mother.

For Germaine Brée, the *Histoire* is a kind of *Bildungsroman* which
traces Sand's successful self-construction beyond the trauma of her
conflicting dependency on her two mothers, both of whom are
accused. According to Brée, Sand picks out and dramatizes as crucial
certain key episodes from her childhood which cast her as innocent
victim and which determined the course of her life. In the first of
these, her grandmother forbade her from seeing her half-sister,
Caroline, during a stay in Paris in an attempt to cut her off from her
maternal family; then her mother, having promised her they would
live together permanently making a modest living running a hat shop,
totally failed to keep her word and abandoned her in Nohant. Later,
in a further attempt to wean her from her passion for her mother, her
grandmother crucially blackened her mother's past and present way of
life, describing her as promiscuous and a fallen woman; and finally
Aurore, having chosen to live with her mother rather than her
aristocratic relatives after her grandmother's death, received only abuse
and rejection. All of these incidents are presented as traumatic,
emotional crises, argues Brée, which threw the young girl back on
herself, made her stronger and eventually forced her into maturity and
independence. It is in her novels that we see the price she had to pay,
concerned as so many of them are with orphans and children who
have been abandoned. For Brée, the writing of the autobiography
was a triumphant act of self-affirmation whereby she transcended
her childhood unhappiness, and rediscovered and forgave her two
mothers: 'Le "moi" de l'autobiographe Sand par ailleurs, tel qu'elle le
reconnaît, est lié à sa victoire sur le conflit personnel et social dont elle
héritait. Les "mères" ont été réconciliées et dépassées, non rejetées,

dans ces scènes d'auto-dramatisation intenses, où l'auto-justification est flagrante.'[18]

Béatrice Didier too sees the *Histoire* as narrating Sand's conquest of her identity against and beyond a series of obstacles, which she defines as 'la famille, l'homme, la société'.[19] But Didier makes more of the positive side of Sand's early attachment to her mother, who is associated with nature, freedom, the imagination and therefore with writing. Thus, in her autobiography, Sand is not only writing herself out of a childhood characterized by deprivation and loss but also rooting herself back in her origins seen as the source of her creativity.

Most of these readings, whether they see her father or her mother as crucial to Sand's self-construction, present the *Histoire* as a success story, which describes and enacts its own completion. Sand is telling her life in terms of its satisfactory end, whereby her double and contradictory identifications are neutralized and resolved. It is also possible, though, to read the *Histoire* as less serenely balanced, less objectively told. By attending to the shifts in linguistic register, the changes in tone and vocabulary, the patterns of imagery, one becomes aware of the presence of a different kind of language which disturbs the uniform surface of calm retrospection. The passion is still there, whether anguished or briefly fulfilled, and always in the context of the girl's mother, not her father or grandmother. Sand never did get over her loss, whatever different strategies she adopted—promiscuity, masculinity, androgyny and writing itself—and it resurfaces perhaps unexpectedly at crucial moments in the narrative. I would agree then with Brée and Didier in placing the mother at the centre of Sand's experience but would argue more strongly that she is still there, haunting the text, in the present telling as well as in the past life, tantalizingly inadequate but inescapable, irremediably absent and yet constantly present at its heart.

Sand first introduces her mother into her autobiography tentatively but also defiantly as though she is breaking some masculine taboo by making much of her maternal inheritance: 'On n'est pas seulement l'enfant de son père, on est aussi un peu, je crois, celui de sa mère. Il me semble même qu'on l'est davantage, et que nous tenons aux entrailles qui nous ont portés, de la façon la plus immédiate, la plus puissante, la plus sacrée' (I, 15). Her defiance here is clearly also the result of her mother's lowly origins, as though heredity is only important if it is aristocratic as well as paternal. It reflects her mother's own pride in her class, 'se sentant peuple jusqu'au bout des ongles'

(I, 501), her refusal to kow-tow and her witty denigration of the 'vieilles comtesses', friends of the older Madame Dupin. This identification with her maternal origins, however obscure (in both senses of the word, as little can be recovered of her mother's heredity), continues throughout Sand's childhood, as she lived it, preferring to run wild with the peasant children at Nohant to behaving like a lady, and as she tells it, for she retrospectively endows her younger self with an egalitarian socialism, a disdain for property of which it is unlikely the child was fully conscious: 'je maudissais le sort qui m'avait fait naître dame et châtelaine contre mon gré. J'enviais la condition des pastours [...]. Je ne voyais dans cette petite fortune, qu'on voulait me faire compter et recompter sans cesse, qu'un embarras dont je ne saurais jamais me tirer, et je ne me trompais nullement' (I, 828). For Sand, poverty and hard work meant and still mean freedom; she idealizes the peasant's life, close to the earth and at one with his community, and she equally celebrates her mother's energy and inventiveness, the active mind and nimble fingers of a working woman. She makes it quite clear that her socialist instincts are the result of her love for and identification with her mother: 'je les dois [...] à mon amour pour ma mère, contrarié et brisé par des préjugés qui m'ont fait souffrir avant que je pusse les comprendre' (I, 629).

Although her mother, born and bred on the streets of Paris, disliked the country, since some of Sand's happiest memories are of their summers together in Nohant she also associates maternity with Nature, with flowers, greenery and running water, all brought together in the grotto which her mother built for her in the garden and which lived on in her memory as an enchanted place: 'Ce n'étaient que cailloux choisis mariant leurs vives couleurs, pierres couvertes de mousses fines et soyeuses, coquillages superbes, festons de lierre au-dessus et gazons tout autour' (I, 633). Significantly too, Sophie was the daughter of a birdseller, so the first mention of her is immediately followed by a long digression on Sand's and her mother's kinship with birds, their maternal care of each other, their intelligence and sense of freedom; this love of birds reappears in her description of her first pregnancy when a robin kept her company at her bedside, thus linking Nature and her mother with her own maternity.

All Sand's innate gifts, she suggests, came to her from her mother: her sensitivity to beautiful things—a wild flower glimpsed in the hedgerows on the journey to Spain or a brightly decorated shop window in Paris—her intuitive religious sense, and most importantly her imagination and talent for story-telling. It was only when she wrote her fantasies down that her mother mocked her, since then they lost their naturalness and simplicity. Her mother allowed her to be herself, to let her mind and body wander freely, unrestrained by reason or convention; of course she was punished sometimes for being too wayward but the punishment was as instinctive and irrational as the bad behaviour. Her bond with her mother is presented as essential, visceral, of the spirit and also of the body; and the vocabulary used to describe it is almost shocking in its violence and physicality—'Il me semblait être attachée physiquement et moralement à ma mère par une chaîne de diamant que ma grand-mère voulait en vain s'efforcer de rompre, et qui ne faisait que se resserrer autour de ma poitrine jusqu'à m'étouffer' (I, 743)—and the child's reaction to her mother's promise of a future together is described equally forcefully: 'Ce beau projet me tourna la tête. J'en eus presque une attaque de nerfs. Je sautais par la chambre en criant et en riant aux éclats, et en même temps je pleurais. J'étais comme ivre' (I, 757–8).

Thus Sand associates all her happiest times with her mother, her summers in Nohant and also her early years in the modest Paris flat, described as a kind of Paradise, briefly recaptured in later visits: 'Et ce petit appartement si pauvre et si laid en comparaison des salons ouatés de ma grand-mère [...] il devint pour moi, en un instant, la terre promise de mes rêves' (I, 660). The only other period of her youth of which she speaks with equal nostalgia are the two years she spent in a convent, where she recaptured that same sense of being enclosed and protected as though in a womb, surrounded by surrogate mothers and sisters. In particular she chose and was chosen by Madame Alicia, one of the nuns, 'mon idéal, mon saint amour, c'était la mère de mon choix' (I, 925), who allowed her to be herself without forfeiting her affection.

Conversely, Sand's greatest suffering also came from her mother, and is described with the same violence, often using direct speech as though the adult narrator is going through the experience again as she tells it. The traumatic scenes picked out by Brée may be the fault of either her grandmother or her mother but are always associated with the threat of separation from the mother to which the child reacts with her whole body, just as she did to the promise of a life of intimacy: 'Ce fut pour moi comme un cauchemar; j'avais la gorge serrée; chaque parole me faisait mourir, je sentais la sueur me couler du front, je voulais interrompre, je voulais me lever, m'en aller, repousser avec horreur cette effroyable confidence; je ne pouvais pas, j'étais clouée sur mes genoux, la tête brisée et courbée par cette voix qui planait sur moi et me desséchait comme un vent d'orage' (I, 856–7).

Her emotional distress can take the form of terrifying dreams and hallucinations. Bozon-Scalzetti sees these as expressions of Aurore's fear of the male and thus the result of an identification with her mother.[20] Certainly the horrific, long-haired figure, who attacks her in her feverish delirium after the crisis of her half-sister's banishment by her grandmother (who clearly stands here for patriarchal law) seems to embody her dread of oppression and annihilation: 'à mesure qu'il tournait il grandissait toujours, il arrivait à la taille d'un homme véritable, jusqu'à ce qu'enfin ce fut [sic] un géant dont les pas rapides frappaient la terre avec bruit, tandis que sa folle chevelure balayait circulairement le plafond avec la légèreté d'une chauve-souris' (I, 654). The nightmare images of her very early childhood when she dreamt that she and her doll were being pursued by a toy Punch, blazing, huge and hostile, or that she was imprisoned inside the gaslight and on fire, seem to express a similar terror which is more fundamental because less clearly motivated. There is an interesting parallel too with the bacchante of the wallpaper who is female but equally terrifying, perhaps reflecting the child's fear of aspects of her two mothers who have merged in her imagination as well as prefiguring her later gender confusions.

After the decisive trauma of the older Madame Dupin's attack on her mother's character, Aurore sank into a state of depression and melancholy, as though her own identity were threatened and she too were guilty: 'je ne m'aimais plus moi-même. Si ma mère était méprisable et haïssable, moi, le fruit de ses entrailles, je l'étais aussi' (I, 858). For years she was overwhelmed by 'un vide affreux, un dégoût, une lassitude de toutes choses et de toutes personnes autour de moi' (I, 1024) which she could survive only by forgetting herself in books, by violent physical exercise or some years later in mad childish games in the family of another substitute mother, Madame du Plessis. But the sadness kept reappearing, to the point of thoughts of suicide. Even after her marriage she did not really recover her capacity to feel, or at least the tone of the *Histoire* remains on the whole reflective and low-key (since it also excludes almost all mention of her platonic passion for Aurélien de Sèze). It is difficult not to attribute this lack of vitality at least in part to the collapse of a sense of self that

went with the loss of her mother, a loss which had been finally
consummated during the period she lived with her in Paris after her
grandmother's death: 'Elle se mit au lit, triomphante de m'avoir
écrasée. Je me retirai dans ma chambre; j'y restai sur une chaise jusqu'au
grand jour, hébétée, ne pensant à rien, sentant mourir mon corps et
mon âme tout ensemble' (I, 1129). It is significant too that she vilifies
her mother while glorifying her grandmother in the long
autobiographical letter she wrote to Aurélien de Sèze in 1825. The
violence of the attack could signify the depth of the distress which she
still felt, and which emerges also in the poignant repetitions at the
beginning of the *Voyage en Auvergne*, written two years later: 'O que
je vous aurais aimée, ma mère, si vous l'aviez voulu! Mais vous m'avez
trahie, vous m'avez menti, ma mère, est-il possible, vous m'avez
menti? Oh que vous êtes coupable! Vous avez brisé mon cœur. Vous
m'avez fait une blessure qui saignera toute la vie' (II, 504). In
describing this period of her life in the *Histoire*, Sand says almost
nothing of the trip to Auvergne, mentioning briefly the beauty of the
countryside and displacing her mental despair onto a sprained ankle,
as the mature, public voice of retrospection takes precedence.

The writing only recovers its passion and energy when dealing with
her arrival in Paris in 1831 to begin a new life after nine years of an
unhappy marriage. Now again it is as though the narrator is reliving
in the present those heady days when she was finally free to do what
she wanted, be who she liked. The style takes off, expressing through
its humour and light-heartedness the happiness of the young woman:
'Je ne peux pas dire quel plaisir me firent mes bottes: j'aurais volontiers
dormi avec, comme fit mon frère dans son jeune âge, quand il chaussa
la première paire. Avec ces petits talons ferrés, j'étais solide sur le
trottoir. Je voltigeais d'un bout de Paris à l'autre. Il me semblait que
j'aurais fait le tour du monde' (II, 117). She is like a character from a
fairy-tale, in disguise, wearing seven-league boots, and Paris is the
enchanted kingdom she is now allowed to enter: 'Je contemplai ce
spectacle de tous les points où je pus me placer, dans les coulisses et
sur la scène, aux loges et au parterre. Je montai à tous les étages: du
club à l'atelier, du café à la mansarde. Il n'y eut que les salons où je
n'eus que faire' (II, 132).

Since her happiness resulted from the freedom acquired by the
donning of men's clothes, it could well be inferred that Sand became
herself by becoming her father, who as a young officer in the late
1790s had also enjoyed the social and artistic life of Paris. However,

her delight in roaming the streets of the city takes us back more explicitly to the earlier descriptions of her walks in Paris as a child with her mother: the same feeling of intoxication, the same wonder at all she sees: 'j'aurais été à pied au bout du monde pour avoir le plaisir de tenir sa main, de toucher sa robe et de regarder avec elle tout ce qu'elle me disait de regarder. Tout me paraissait beau à travers ses yeux. Les boulevards étaient un lieu enchanté' (I, 648). In exploring Paris, in exchanging the quiet spaces of Nohant for the bustle and bright lights of the town, Aurore is both going back to happy moments of her early years, and also reintegrating her mother's own past as a street-wise city girl. Indeed it was in imitation of her mother and at her suggestion that she put on men's clothes in order to go where she liked, to theatres and cafés, unremarked and anonymous, and it was also of her mother she thought when casting around for ways of earning her living. She associates her independence then with a woman, her mother, not the gentleman nor yet the lady (her father and grandmother) who were her two alternative role models: 'Je n'étais plus une *dame*, je n'étais pas non plus un *monsieur*' (II, 135). She had already worn men's clothes for riding in Nohant but the liberation transvestism had brought her then was purely practical; now, although she plays down its sexually disturbing aspects, it clearly transformed her more fundamentally, allowing her through identification with her maternal origins to take on a new persona.

Not that this persona was consistently sustained or untroubled. Her contradictory identities were not so easily resolved, and her success in Paris as a professional writer was quickly followed by a depression and anxiety, described as philosophical in the retrospective *Histoire* but expressed also, perhaps more authentically, in the sexually ambiguous figure of *Lélia*, written in 1833. Her mother now disappears from the autobiography, re-emerging only several years later in order to die, provoking the mature Sand into a balanced reassessment of their relationship. She brings out the strongly physical response she still felt to their occasional meetings but the factual, dispassionate tone in which she briefly narrates her death (although somewhat contradicted by contemporary letters) suggests that the feeling was numbed or suppressed, that Sand had mourned her loss so repeatedly and with such intensity as a young girl that there was nothing left to say; it is the grief of Pierret, her mother's companion, that she describes rather than her own.

What of Sand's father in all this? Is this preoccupation with her mother balanced by the many pages devoted to his antecedents and his youth? Is it because she could not describe his presence in her life that she felt the need to fill out in such detail his past before she was born, as a way of incorporating him into her own existence, to fill in a blank? In view of her determined rejection of her aristocratic inheritance in the present as well as in the past, 'cette caste à laquelle mes entrailles tiennent beaucoup moins directement qu'au ventre de ma mère',[21] as she called it in 1843, it seems odd that she should make so much of it in her autobiography. She may simply be obeying the conventions of the genre: for example she says that she only includes a full portrait of her great-grandfather, Maurice de Saxe, at the request of her readers, and then she reproduces an extract from a history book upon which she comments. She is muted in her praise of him, and dislikes and feels accused by the picture of Aurore de Kœnigsmark, his mother. Her attempt to give herself the roots she did not really feel is distinctly ambiguous. She interestingly makes the point that it is on her mother's side that she is legitimate: both her grandmother and her great-grandfather were natural children. She tries to reincorporate her father into her own story by stressing the liberalism, the enthusiasm for republican ideas which they shared and which he demonstrated most clearly in his love for her mother, the genuine intensity of which she repeatedly emphasizes. It is of course with this aspect of his life that she finds it easiest to empathize, hence the lengthy quoting of his letters. The identification, though, is still indirect, second-hand, and the language she uses to rewrite the letters is somewhat studied and unconvincing, the style of a sentimental novel, not of lived experience. She herself admits in a letter that it was only when she reached her own childhood (from which he was largely absent) that her writing came to life: 'C'est presque un prodige comme mes souvenirs d'enfance se réveillent à mesure que j'approche de l'époque où je vais parler de moi.'[22] His death is a blank; she only describes her mother's anguish, and the black stockings she was forced to wear. It was retrospectively and therefore rationally that she realized how utterly his death had changed the course of her life.

Her father, then, is barely remembered, largely an absence, inadequately if lengthily filled by conscious idealization. In her life she had two substitute fathers but they have none of the aura and efficacy of the substitute mothers. Both are described as comic figures, inspiring affection but neither admiration nor respect. The first is Pierret, her mother's lifelong friend and companion, who oddly took over the maternal rather than the paternal role by being the one to wean the baby Aurore from the breast. The other is Deschartres, her eccentric tutor and manager of the estate at Nohant, who brought her up as though she were a boy and as he had done her father, but whom she and her half-brother cruelly mocked as children and whom she still cannot take very seriously. It was of course her grandmother who took the father's place, without being either father or male, and as a result the portrait of her which emerges is interestingly contradictory.

Sand's description of her first remembered meeting with her grandmother prefigures and defines their relationship throughout the rest of her childhood. Her family had just arrived at Nohant, exhausted and ill (she had scabies), after a horrific journey from Madrid through the battlefields of Spain. Madame Dupin received them at her door:

Elle me parut très grande, quoiqu'elle n'eût que cinq pieds, et sa figure blanche et rosée, son air imposant, son invariable costume composé d'une robe de soie brune à taille longue et à manches plates, qu'elle n'avait pas voulu modifier selon les exigences de la mode de l'Empire, sa perruque blonde et crêpée en touffe sur le front, son petit bonnet rond avec une cocarde de dentelle au milieu, firent d'elle pour moi un être à part et qui ne ressemblait en rien à ce que j'avais vu. (I, 585)

She immediately took charge of Aurore: 'Gale ou non, dit ma grand-mère en me serrant contre son cœur, je me charge de celui-là' (I, 586). She never wavered in her sense of responsibility for the child, just as the child was unable to get over her awe, to bridge the distance between them. As an adult, Sand plays down her grandmother's womanliness, presents her as having never known passion for a man (apart from her all-consuming love for her son), as strict, chaste, asexual. She is a product of the eighteenth century in her refinement and reserve, and also in her rationalism. A follower of Voltaire, she only went through the forms of Catholicism for the sake of convention and to please her grand-daughter. She provoked in the young Aurore 'une sorte de vénération morale jointe à un éloignement physique invincible' (I, 640). Their temperaments were totally opposed: 'C'était une nature si calme, si régulière, si unie, qu'elle ne comprenait pas les engouements et les défaillances de la mienne' (I, 843–4). According to Sand, she found it difficult to accept the child as she was, but wished perhaps quite naturally to mould her into a young lady who would fit into the aristocratic circles in which (as she thought) her grand-daughter was to move. She disliked her running wild, or indeed running at all, and tried to train her to behave at all times with restraint and decorum, wishing to counteract what she saw as 'une sorte de vice originel qui sentait le peuple en dépit de tous ses soins' (I, 942). The child felt her influence and presence as threatening her very existence: 'J'avais une peur effroyable de devenir comme elle, et quand elle m'ordonnait de n'être à ses côtés ni agitée ni bruyante, il me semblait qu'elle me commandât d'être morte' (I, 640).

Indeed significantly at several key points in the text, her actions are given as killing a primary source of happiness in the young Aurore. First, she had the garden grotto built by her mother destroyed, unable to understand its magic. Later, she banished the child from her mother's bed, seeing their physical intimacy as unhealthy, just as she had excluded her half-sister, Caroline, from her house; and then, most brutally (as we have seen), she destroyed her mother's reputation beyond recall, causing something fundamental to die in the young girl: 'je ne pensais plus, je ne vivais pas, j'étais indifférente à toutes choses. Je ne savais plus si j'aimais ou si je haïssais quelqu'un, je ne sentais plus d'enthousiasme pour personne, plus de ressentiment contre qui que ce soit; j'avais comme une énorme brûlure intérieure et comme un vide cuisant à la place du cœur' (I, 858). Then finally she removed Aurore from the convent where she was happy, removed her abruptly and without warning, fearing the power of the girl's newly found religious faith: 'Cette nouvelle tomba sur moi comme un coup de foudre, au milieu du plus parfait bonheur que j'eusse goûté de ma vie' (I, 1007).

She appears, then, largely as a source of pain: the child felt her influence as the opposite of her mother's and reacted accordingly, oppressed and withdrawn, rather than blossoming into life. However, alongside this negative picture of her grandmother and in a way overlaying it, there are many passages in the *Histoire* where Sand retrospectively insists on her fine qualities, just as, as an adult, she was able to see her mother's many faults. The mature woman understood how much she owed her grandmother, her constant care, her pre-occupation with her education, her concern for her future, and uses her autobiography to acknowledge the debt. She affirms that she now cherishes her two mothers equally, able to understand them both and allot praise and blame in a true spirit of justice. Yet is the reader entirely convinced? Rationally, yes, we see that the older Madame Dupin was a more admirable person than her daughter-in-law, that it was she who gave Sand the security to grow into what she became, capable, independent and hard-working, but the tone of these passages is sober and dutiful, clearly the conscious voice of the older narrator rather than the spontaneous cry of the child.

Past and present, emotion and reflection, coexist then in the text, and we also see described there the change from the one to the other, the process of maturing which weaned Sand away from her passion for her mother to a more sober affection for her grandmother. We see her lose faith in her mother's love and turn increasingly to that calmer, more deliberate appreciation of the older Madame Dupin, which characterizes the conscious narrating voice of the *Histoire*. The turning point occurred during the year and a half Aurore spent in Nohant after she had left the convent and before her grandmother's death, when the young girl was left much alone: 'J'étais frappée d'un grand respect en même temps que d'une tendre gratitude pour l'intention qu'elle avait eue de me complaire' (I, 1069). The change is expressed interestingly as a reversal of roles. In nursing her grandmother through her long, final illness, Aurore became a kind of mother to her, and began to feel that visceral attachment which for her characterized the maternal bond, as though it was only through this relationship that she could feel strongly at all: 'Un jour vint où nous changeâmes de rôle, et où je sentis pour elle une tendresse des entrailles qui ressemblait aux sollicitudes de la maternité' (I, 1025). The emotion is transient, though, and to some extent illusory, and her grandmother's clear-sighted, final words to her on her deathbed '*Tu perds ta meilleure amie*' (I, 1106) define more accurately what their relationship was and how Sand herself came to see it. She is able to acknowledge too that her grandmother never got over the loss of her son and that she herself was never more than a substitute for him. Thus, at her death, described quite soberly, she says she felt no more than 'une tristesse paisible' (I, 1108).

Sand's lack of a father and abandonment by her mother combined with her grandmother's suspicion of physical intimacy to induce in her a fear of sex together with a longing for love which may well explain her future androgyny, largely preferring the masculine and maternal (as also in her relations with her lovers) to the overtly sexual. She describes in the *Histoire* how as a child she invented an imaginary, ideal figure, Corambé,[23] to compensate for her loneliness and people her emotional void, and his importance is clearly implied by the length and poignancy of her account. He was to fulfil her every need: 'je voulais l'aimer comme un ami, comme une sœur en même temps que le révérer comme un dieu' (I, 813) (in place of her absent father), but most crucially he was a substitute for her mother: 'Et puis, il me fallait le compléter en le vêtant en femme à l'occasion, car ce que j'avais le mieux aimé, le mieux compris jusqu'alors, c'était une femme, c'était ma mère' (I, 813). Male and female, half human, half divine, he arose out of her unconscious, nourished by images from pagan mythology and the Bible, and took over her imagination completely. Mediator and consoler, he became the centre of her fantasy life, as she wove endless stories around him in her mind. She built him an altar in the garden at Nohant (clearly reminiscent of the grotto built for her by her mother), where she brought him offerings of birds, butterflies and insects which she then set free: 'Je crois que j'étais devenue un peu comme ce pauvre fou qui cherchait la tendresse. Je la demandais aux bois, aux plantes, au soleil, aux animaux, et à je ne sais quel être invisible qui n'existait que dans mes rêves' (I, 820).

Unable, she says, to imagine any kind of romantic, sexual attachment as most young girls do, the cult of Corambé satisfied her need for love, but non-corporeally, beyond gender distinctions and therefore safely. He disappeared for a while after her grandmother's assassination of her mother's character, demonstrating the depths of despair into which she had fallen, and his place was briefly taken after her conversion at the convent by Christ, whom she also describes as a substitute for her mother and as an ideal father, but he was never completely forgotten. Sand presents her marriage too as un-threatening, safe, although ultimately unsatisfying. She saw her future husband not as a sexual partner but as a good companion, a friend, and she was able to agree to marry him only on these terms: 'Je crois qu'à l'époque de ma vie où je me trouvais, et au sortir de si grandes irrésolutions entre le couvent et la famille, une passion brusque m'eût épouvantée' (II, 27). It is true that the letters she wrote to Casimir in the early years after their marriage express a certain passion and desire for intimacy (perhaps in keeping with what she felt was expected of a young wife, or perhaps sincerely) but there is no sign of this in the *Histoire*. He is only mentioned briefly in so far as he turned out not to understand her and so not to be the companion she had hoped for.

At least retrospectively, then, it seems as though he hardly impinged on her inner life, and was no help in leading her out of her emotional impasse.

Sand states clearly that it was only years after her marriage, when she began writing her first novel, that Corambé finally disappeared, implying that both answered the same need in her. This places the compulsion to write at a much deeper level than she usually admits to: it is much more than a convenient way of earning a living or even a craft for which she happens to have some facility. It is linked closely to her emotional development, intertwined with her past experiences and present state of mind, a way of going beyond and resolving the gender contradictions of her childhood. This is perhaps truer of her fiction than of her autobiography, more obviously the product of conscious reminiscence than unconscious dreams. The distinction, though, has long been recognized as spurious; through its selectivity, its reliance on involuntary as well as voluntary memories, its patterns of imagery and changing linguistic registers, the *Histoire* is also revealing of Sand's hidden inner life. Her control of the text is by no means total. The picture of herself which emerges may go beyond what she intended, may uncover more than she might have wished, even if we are sceptical of readings that are too closely Freudian. Thus she may be presenting herself as asexual, neutrally and universally typical, not just to preempt hostile criticism but also as a result of the same (too feminine) fears and desires that had led to the emergence of Corambé and which are still there, only partially suppressed or resolved.

Notes to Chapter 2

1. See Richard Coe, *When the Grass was Taller: Autobiography and the Experience of Childhood* (New Haven: Yale University Press, 1984), 140.
2. Sigmund Freud, *Beyond the Pleasure Principle* (1920), in *The Essentials of Psycho-Analysis* (Harmondsworth: Penguin Books, 1991), 227.
3. Sigmund Freud, 'Femininity', *New Introductory Lectures on Psychoanalysis* (1933) (Harmondsworth: Penguin Books, 1991), 417.
4. Freud, 'Femininity', 416.
5. Nancy Chodorow, *The Reproduction of Mothering: Psychoanalysis and the Sociology of Gender* (Berkeley: University of California Press, 1978), 136.
6. Virginia Woolf, *A Room of One's Own* (London: HarperCollins, Flamingo, 1994), 83.
7. Celeste M. Schenck and Bella Brodski (eds.), *Life/Lines: Theorizing Women's Autobiography* (Ithaca: Cornell University Press, 1988), 245–6.

8. See Gilbert and Gubar, *The Madwoman in the Attic*, 17.

9. Lucienne Frappier-Mazur, 'Nostalgie, dédoublement et écriture dans *Histoire de ma vie*', *Nineteenth-Century French Studies* (Spring–Summer 1989), 267.

10. Deutsch, *The Psychology of Women*, 248.

11. Crecelius, *Family Romances*, 21.

12. Crecelius, *Family Romances*, 9.

13. Schor, *George Sand and Idealism*, 174.

14. To be compared with Daniel Stern's adoration of her father as presented in *Mes Souvenirs*.

15. Schor, *George Sand and Idealism*, 179.

16. See Marianne Hirsch, *The Mother/Daughter Plot* (Bloomington: Indiana University Press, 1989).

17. Yvette Bozon-Scalzetti, 'Vérité de la fiction et fiction de la vérité dans *Histoire de ma vie*', *Nineteenth-Century French Studies* (Summer–Fall 1984), 95.

18. Germaine Brée, 'Le Mythe des origines et l'autoportrait chez George Sand et Colette', in *Studies in honour of Wallace Fowlie*, ed. Marcel Tetel (Durham, North Carolina: Duke University Press, 1978), 108.

19. Béatrice Didier, 'Femme, identité, écriture: à propos de *Histoire de ma vie* de George Sand', *Revue des Sciences humaines* 42 (Oct.–Dec. 1977), 563.

20. Bozon-Scalzetti, 'Vérité de la fiction'.

21. Sand, *Correspondance*, vi. 328.

22. Sand, *Correspondance*, viii. 264.

23. Helene Deutsch explains the name, Corambé, as being made up of 'coram', 'in the presence of', and 'bé', the letter b, which Sand refused to learn as a child and which according to Deutsch signifies the absent father whose loss Sand had repressed. Sand herself denied that the name meant anything at all.

CHAPTER 3

Structure

The structure of an autobiography is inevitably defined to some extent by the temporal shape of a life; even the most modernist texts whose techniques of fragmentation and simultaneity play freely with chronology still have time as a basic reference point, and it is this consciousness of 'our life in time and our mortality that generates much of the impulse to write autobiography'.[1] All lives go through the same set of experiences, moving from childhood through adolescence to maturity, and contain similar key discoveries—of the self as separate, of evil, sex and death.[2] Through the retrospective telling of these experiences, an autobiographer transforms them into a narrative and gives them meaning and coherence as stages in the construction of an identity. This is the implication of Philippe Lejeune's definition of an autobiography as the story of a personality,[3] and Patricia Spacks too talks of 'the structure of cause and effect'[4] imposed on a life by making it into a text.

The most common shape given to a destiny, whether real or fictional, in the positivist nineteenth century was of course that of the *Bildungsroman* which plots the successful quest for a self in the world and the discovery of a vocation. Roy Pascal sees this as a kind of model autobiography: 'All good autobiographies are in some sense the story of a calling', the most successful being those by writers and artists.[5] We have already seen how Brée likens Sand's *Histoire de ma vie* to a *Bildungsroman* as the text narrates her journey through life via certain significant and highly dramatized episodes culminating in her departure to Paris and her triumphant assumption of an identity and a vocation. Julia Watson makes the same comparison: 'The voluminous autobiography of George Sand (Aurore Dupin Dudevant) uses several modes of literary fiction to present her life as a fable for instructing and educating the reader, much as a *bildungsroman* might.'[6]

The structure of such a traditional autobiography has as its basis the

'authentic' memories of the writer which he/she uses as stepping
stones in the tracing of the plot, deliberately arranging them into
a temporal sequence even though this denies their simultaneous
coexistence in the present consciousness of the narrator. Sheringham
distinguishes between 'domesticated' incidents which take their
necessary and logical place in the development of the narrative, and
those he terms 'wild', whose significance is less clear to the writer but
which he includes and reflects on out of a genuine need to understand
himself.[7] Remembered incidents can also signify independently of
their surface meaning, having their roots in unconscious obsessions,
present as well as past, for which they act as screens.[8] Thus the main
narrative line is given depth, a sense of the mystery and possible
incoherence of a life preserved, and the imagination of the reader is
stirred to wonder and to dream. Sand's description of the *Histoire* as
'une série de souvenirs, de professions de foi et de méditations'[9] sets
up an idea of sequence, but filled out and disrupted by the present
reflections of the author; and the narrative itself draws us along a chain
of associated memories whose vividness may sometimes seem out of
proportion with their apparent significance.

Most often, though, Sand, like Germaine Brée, sees her narrative
as a traditional *Bildungsroman*, insisting retrospectively on its logic,
offering various keys to her development at different points. Heredity
is presented as fundamental, complemented by certain critical
experiences: the death of her father, the conflict between her mother
and grandmother for control of her life, her eccentric education by
her tutor Deschartres and her voracious reading alone at Nohant, her
choice of her mother after her grandmother's death which led to
rejection by her aristocratic relatives and her rush into an early,
unsatisfactory marriage and finally her crucial decision nine years later
to leave for Paris. She frequently identifies turning points and
moments of choice, making the reader increasingly aware of her
dreaminess as a child, her unusual upbringing, her alienation from
local society and her difference from other young women of her class.
Not that she ever suggests the advantages of such a training for a girl
(as we shall see, she stresses her suffering and loneliness), but she does
recognize the tendency towards introspection and independence of
mind which it fostered in her and which made her what she
eventually became. She presents her personality as 'le résultat
inévitable de mes premières douleurs, de mes plus saintes affections,
de ma situation même dans la vie' (I, 781). Later, as she moves into an

account of her politicization, she adds a further dimension to her story, describing her development from an excessive concern with herself to an awareness of others and a sense of solidarity with the world. It is from this final perspective that she is writing. The basic structure of the *Histoire* is, then, chronological and teleological, purposeful and determined, to fit in with the way a man (rather than a woman) is said to live his life, and Sand is certainly writing within this (male) tradition. However, there are certain features of the text which are at odds with this view, which cast doubt on its linearity and predictability. Sand also draws attention to these: 'Je pourrai donc parler sans ordre et sans suite, tomber même dans beaucoup de contradictions. La nature humaine n'est qu'un tissu d'inconséquences, et je ne crois point du tout (mais du tout) à ceux qui prétendent s'être toujours trouvés d'accord avec le *moi* de la veille' (I, 13). Of course, there are many autobiographies by men which do not have the order and logic that an over-simplified polarization would imply, including *Vie de Henri Brulard* by Sand's own contemporary, Stendhal. But the particular kinds of disruption we find in the *Histoire* do appear closely linked to the structural differences which theorists have noticed in texts by women, and which they attribute to their gender and specific life experience.

Undoubtedly the most fundamental of these concerns the primary plot of a woman's story. It is easy to see how much less readily a woman's life takes on the shape of a quest basic to a traditional autobiography, and so how much more difficult it was, particularly in the early nineteenth century, for her to write about herself as active and central. Conventional views of a woman's role fitted more easily within the romance plot where her place was clearly subordinate to man's desire and her only possible end annihilation through either marriage or death.[10] Sand attempts to conflate the quest with the romance plot in some of her novels, offering as the final resolution of the heroine's search an equal and therefore idealized, spiritual relationship with a man, but the strange, mystical endings of both *Indiana* and *Consuelo* demonstrate the difficulties this solution posed, which she could only resolve by removing her characters entirely from the real world. When she came to write her own life, she lost the freedom fiction gave her to reinvent herself, to recast her life in alternative directions which would test the heroine in new and exciting ways even if the end proved problematic. An autobiographer, man or woman, is at least partly constrained by the facts, and since the facts are that a woman is unlikely to have carved out an independent role for herself without considerable difficulty, without a number of false starts, the text which tries to give coherence and meaning to her life will also be more tentative, take longer to get going and give more sense of the alternative stories it might have told. Turning points may be undercut, shown not to be turning points at all or to have turned the protagonist in the wrong direction. Women's texts are said to be more personal, digressive, non-chronological. 'The heroine's developmental course is more conflicted, less direct; separation tugs against the longing for fusion.'[11] And yet beneath all this, beneath the twists and turns of a destiny which cannot find itself, the thread remains, the story moves on and forward to a conclusion of a kind. In accordance with such a view, Sand's *Histoire* needs to be studied from two different perspectives—to show how it conforms to a well-established pattern, but how that pattern is at the same time obscured and questioned.

Let us look first at Sand's account of her childhood. Here the sense of logical sequence is clear; the successive stages through which she passed give us the same feeling of coherence and growth that we find in numerous other narratives of a life, whether actual or theoretical. Since no autobiographer can remember being born, the origin, the awakening to the world, is conventionally displaced onto the first memory, which, emerging from a sea of darkness, is made to prefigure symbolically the life to come. Sand's first memory is of being dropped by a maid at the age of 2:

J'avais deux ans, une bonne me laissa tomber de ses bras sur l'angle d'une cheminée, j'eus peur et je fus blessée au front. Cette commotion, cet ébranlement du système nerveux ouvrirent mon esprit au sentiment de la vie, et je vis nettement, je vois encore, le marbre rougeâtre de la cheminée, mon sang qui coulait, la figure égarée de ma bonne. Je me rappelle distinctement aussi la visite du médecin, les sangsues qu'on me mit derrière l'oreille, l'inquiétude de ma mère, et la bonne congédiée pour cause d'ivrognerie. (I, 530)

Here we witness the child's first apprehension of the difference between herself and others.[12] We might also stress the sense of shock, the emotional distress rather than physical pain which coincides with this coming to consciousness of the self in a décor of blood and reddish marble. Bozon-Scalzetti convincingly sees this incident as representative of the first of many abandonments.[13] Here the young Aurore is literally let down by the adult who should be caring for her, and the later emotional let-downs perhaps explain why she still relives in its every detail that first traumatic fall.

Sand then moves immediately into an account of her early idyllic years with her mother and half-sister in the flat in the rue Grange-Batelière: 'De là datent mes souvenirs précis et presque sans interruption' (I, 530), she says, although we may feel that certain intense experiences alone have survived, all of them suggestive of a childhood steeped in a sense of the marvellous and the supernatural. She lists a number of vividly felt, isolated memories—of nursery rhymes sung to her by her mother, of frightening dreams and hallucinations, of the white dress of a little girl taking her first communion and, particularly privileged, of the sound of a flute echoing in the sky over the rooftops of Paris. Throughout, the emphasis is on the child's imagination, her dreaminess, the fantasy world in which she lived and which poured out in the endless stories she told herself, while standing in her makeshift playpen with her mother working beside her and sometimes joining in to help her recapture the thread. Sand herself makes the link between these interminable inventions and the 'laisser-aller invincible' (I, 542) of her present writing practice. Although Aurore is 2 or 3 years old by now and has acquired some kind of infantile language, there does seem to be a similarity between this account of the child's symbiotic closeness with her mother in the world of the imagination, and the pre-Oedipal stage in Freud, and Lacan's concept of the Imaginary, both often seen as more prolonged for the little girl than the little boy. Sand also ties these early years clearly into the original Judeo-Christian myth of a paradise lost by describing them as 'cet âge d'or comme un rêve évanoui, auquel rien ne saurait être comparé dans la suite' (I, 529). Here then her story coincides with certain archetypal narrative schemes so that it makes sense both in its own terms and in terms of a more general experience.

A universal pattern appears again in her description of the next stage in her development on whose importance she insists. This took place during the brief period of two months which the child spent with her family in Madrid as they followed her father during his service under Murat in Napoleon's army. It is here that she repeatedly experienced what Frappier-Mazur calls 'des phénomènes de dédoublement'[14] through which she acquired a sense of herself as other, as she might be perceived from the outside. This was the first time she had been left alone without her mother for long periods, and more importantly the first time she saw herself in a full-length mirror, in front of which with her pet rabbit in her arms she performed all kinds of mimes and impersonations: 'Alors j'oubliais complètement que cette figure dansant dans la glace fût la mienne, et j'étais étonnée qu'elle s'arrétât quand je m'arrêtais' (I, 572). Again, although Aurore is now nearly 4 years old and the mirror is a common image of self-awareness, her experience seems very close to Lacan's mirror stage, described by Susan Sellers: 'According to Lacan, the child's recognition of its mirror-image coincides with its growing sense of itself as external to and separate from the m/other as well as its first attempts at self-expression.'[15] As before, we can also see a link with Sand's later literary creativity as the child invents and acts out impromptu stories to herself.

This experience of doubling, this discovery of the self as both subject and object, is then immediately reinforced by Aurore's hearing the echo of her own voice as she called out to her father's servant on the huge terrace of the palace in which they lived: 'Alors il me vint à l'esprit une explication bizarre. C'est que j'étais double, et qu'il y avait autour de moi un autre *moi* que je ne pouvais pas voir, mais qui me voyait toujours, puisqu'il me répondait toujours' (I, 573). Since she has also just been struck by the image of the golden globe and cross of the church opposite which remained on her retina even when she was looking elsewhere, she concludes that everything has its double, and this convinces her further of her own dual existence.

Aurore takes one more step in her growing awareness of her situation in the world during this crucially formative stay in Madrid. Until then, she says, she had little sense of the existence of others; 'la vie du sentiment' (I, 575) had no meaning for her. However, on seeing her mother's suffering caused by the birth of her baby brother, the child suddenly makes the leap of imagination which enables her to feel with her beloved mother in her weakened state: 'Ma mère était étendue sur un canapé, elle avait la figure si pâle et les traits tellement contractés, que j'hésitai à la reconnaître. Puis, je fus prise d'un grand effroi et je courus l'embrasser en pleurant' (I, 575). Although the baby boy was born blind, it is significant that it is her love for her mother, not pity for her brother (to whom she remains indifferent), which awakens Aurore to the world of feeling.

Shortly after the family's flight from Madrid and arrival in Nohant in September 1808, both the baby and Sand's father died, within ten days of each other. The adult narrator makes clear the catastrophic effect the second of these deaths had on her life: 'j'en ai ressenti le contrecoup toute ma vie' (I, 594), but Aurore's horrified apprehension of the fact of death, another crucial stage in a child's development, is displaced by Sand back to an incident, already described, when she was travelling through war-torn Spain with her mother to join her father in Madrid. She had been given a pigeon to play with whose constant attempts to fly away had disappointed her caresses. She had then asked for it to be killed, not knowing what the word meant, and so had been taken to the kitchen to witness the putting to death of the other pigeons which were to be served up for the family's supper. It was at this point that the child is said to have realized the difference between life and death, since she was later offered the dead pigeons to eat. As we saw earlier, she records little reaction to her father's death, says she expected him to come back soon, and we are never told whether or not she missed him.

The emphasis of the next 250 pages is on the second, more important separation, from the mother, which in the *Histoire* is made to appear far more protracted than it was in reality. To begin with, Sand extends to two or three years the few months during which she was torn between her mother and grandmother in Nohant. Secondly, after her mother left for Paris in 1809, Sand repeatedly stresses the happiness of the summers when she briefly returned and played with her daughter in the garden or read to her the stories of Madame de Genlis while the child sat dreaming in front of the fire, so recapturing that same world of the imagination which they had shared in her early years in the Paris flat. The summer of 1811 is described as 'une des rares époques de ma vie où je connus le bonheur complet' (I, 687), coming after what Sand calls 'un apprentissage du malheur et de la souffrance' (I, 688). The summers of both 1812 and 1813, she says, were equally tranquilly spent with her mother, but her grandmother's letters prove that her mother actually remained for these years in Paris. In this way, the account of her traumatic abandonment is deferred while also being constantly anticipated: 'C'était en effet la fin de mon bonheur qui approchait' (I, 732); and this has the effect of magnifying its importance since by the time it is actually described, it had long been consummated in reality. When Sand finally comes to relate the anguished night the child spent before what she saw as her mother's definitive departure in the summer of 1814 (although she was to return in 1815), she dramatizes it considerably, making it bear the full weight of a distress which in reality was much more diffused. She transforms into a long, passionate cry of despair the farewell letter the young Aurore wrote to her mother, which actually consisted of a few simple lines, and quite clearly sets the incident up as a first Fall into an awareness of suffering and loss from which she never recovered: 'c'était la première aube que je voyais paraître après une nuit de douleur et d'insomnie. Combien d'autres depuis, que je ne saurais compter!' (I, 761).

Her second Fall was to come three years later when her grandmother told her of her mother's dubious past; this time it is a Fall into an awareness of sin and sex. It appears like a version of the Oedipal crisis, but without the father who would have compensated for her loss. Although accompanied by descriptions of the child's pleasure as she ran wild with the children of the estate and listened to the stories told in the evening by the 'chanvreurs', the pain and loneliness of the intervening period are again constantly and oddly reiterated. Sand had already made much of them after the separation of 1814, as though things could hardly get worse:

je me sentis, je me trouvai malheureuse, et c'était l'être en réalité. Je m'habituais même à goûter une sorte d'amère satisfaction à protester intérieurement et à toute heure contre cette destinée, à m'obstiner de plus en plus à n'aimer qu'un être absent et qui semblait m'abandonner à ma misère [...] enfin à me regarder comme un pauvre être exceptionnellement voué à l'esclavage, à l'injustice, à l'ennui et à d'éternels regrets. (I, 780–1)

But when her brother goes off to join his regiment at the beginning of 1816, they do: 'Alors s'écoulèrent pour moi les deux plus longues, les deux plus rêveuses, les deux plus mélancoliques années qu'il y eût encore eu [sic] dans ma vie' (I, 798). Then in a kind of recapitulation, it is the last four years which are said to have been crucial in her moral and physical development as she retreated into the fantasy world of her imagination, and Corambé made his appearance. Finally, as we have seen, she suffered a kind of moral and physical death after the climactic scene with her grandmother who told her 'des choses qui ne se disent qu'une fois dans la vie, parce qu'elles ne s'oublient pas' (I, 855). From these depths the young Aurore is only rescued by being sent off to a convent.

It is at this point that Sand's story becomes more characteristically the story of a young girl living in the early nineteenth century, since for many daughters of the upper classes at that time a few years in a convent (and the Couvent des Augustines was particularly fashionable) were an essential part of their education, and since of course a convent environment is exclusively and intensely female. Indeed, Madame Dupin's intention in sending her granddaughter there was explicitly to make her into a 'lady' (I, 861). This is also the point at which several alternative endings to her story are suggested as we are told how the young girl played out to extremes her opposing identities in the safety and seclusion of the convent, the closing of whose doors upon her for over two years she effectively dramatizes: 'on ouvrit une porte de communication qui se referma derrière nous. J'étais cloîtrée' (I, 862). She began by playing the 'diable', as she puts it, acting as ringleader to a group of rebels, Sand here anticipating a long tradition of girls' school stories, complete with midnight feasts and passionate, girlish friendships, of which those by Angela Brazil are a kind of archetype. One of their preferred escapades was to slip away from the classroom in the evening in order to range through the labyrinthine passages and cellars of the huge convent building to rescue a supposed victim who they imagined had been incarcerated in its depths for years. A link is made here with Ann Radcliffe's Gothic romances (I, 887), and the Gothic is often seen as a woman's genre, expressive of a woman's fantasies and nightmares. It was to reappear later in some of Sand's novels, in particular in *Consuelo*, but crucially reversed since here the 'damsel in distress' is a young man who is discovered and rescued by the heroine.

In the convent, though, it was all fun, make-believe, a safe way of testing limits. The opposite extreme, to which the young Aurore swung when these adventures began to pall, had potentially more serious consequences since her conversion to an intense Christian faith almost led to her becoming a nun. Again, the conversion is clearly presented as derivative, as an imitation of the lives of the Saints which Aurore began to read out of boredom and which quickly gripped her imagination, and in particular of the *Confessions* of St Augustine whose 'Tolle, lege' she enacts to the letter. Although, as we shall see, the actual moment of conversion appears miraculous, an unpredicted epiphany, there seems to be a certain unconscious deliberateness about the original intention, as though the young girl is searching for an example to follow, a model for her life which will satisfy her need for intense fulfilment as well as for a clear sense of direction. Sand refers to other nuns' stories: she compares her young self to St Teresa, gives an account of the exemplary life of her friend, Sœur Hélène, the simple lay sister who fanatically sought out martyrdom; she tells us of or ᵉ of her convent friends who did become a nun, and even gives us a rapid view of how she herself might have turned out if her confessor had been less perceptive and sensible in the advice he gave her: 'Sans lui, je crois bien que je serais ou folle, ou religieuse cloîtrée à l'heure qu'il est' (I, 963). And of course the most acceptable 'quest plot' for a woman until that time had hinged on a religious conversion leading to a life of mysticism and devotion.

This could then have been the end of Aurore Dupin's story. It turned out very quickly, however, to be a false turn since she overdid the asceticism, became ill and returned to a more normal life, in which indeed she briefly achieved a kind of balance (significantly as director of stage performances of Molière by the convent girls) and was totally happy, before her abrupt removal from the convent by her grandmother. In the end, her two years there proved to be a kind of digression, an irrelevance, a pause in her life which led nowhere (she says she learned very little and quickly lost touch with most of her convent friends), just as the lengthy descriptions she includes of the convent buildings and the different personalities who inhabited them provide a pause in the narrative, as she says (I, 870). This period of her life acted as 'une sorte de halte au milieu de la lutte que je subissais' (I, 862), during which she lived out of time, entirely in the present; it did not perform the expected transition into adulthood, for she became neither an aristocratic lady nor a nun.

A traditional ending to her story had already been offered her by her spiritual mother, Madame Alicia, who was suspicious of her vocation and predicted for her a future as wife and mother. All her relatives, aristocratic and plebeian, agreed, which suggests that Sand as narrator is wrong in setting up her choice of her mother after her grandmother's death as crucial since we can see retrospectively that a conventional marriage was unlikely to have satisfied her whoever her husband had been and from whatever class. Two years later, in 1822, at the age of 18, Aurore did marry Casimir Dudevant, a retired army officer and a member of the petty aristocracy, clearly if unconsciously influenced by the happy conjugality between Monsieur and Madame Du Plessis at whose house she met him, and in obvious pursuit of their idyllic family life which she had never known for herself and which she celebrates at length in the *Histoire* without directly presenting it as a motivation.

It was too late, however, a critical two years too late, since the time the adolescent Aurore had spent alone at Nohant between the convent and her marriage, in the company of her now remote and ailing grandmother, had marked her out from other young girls and altered her for ever, unfitting her for a traditional woman's ending:

Si ma destinée m'eût fait passer immédiatement de la domination de ma grand-mère à celle d'un mari ou à celle du couvent, il est possible que, soumise toujours à des influences acceptées, je n'eusse jamais été moi-même […]. Mais il était décidé par le sort que dès l'âge de dix-sept ans il y aurait pour moi un temps d'arrêt dans les influences extérieures, et que je m'appartiendrais entièrement pendant près d'une année, pour devenir, en bien ou en mal, ce que je devais être à peu près tout le reste de ma vie.' (I, 1033)

Left to herself, Aurore read everything she could find, 'le tout sans ordre et sans méthode' (I, 1051), philosophy, theology, as well as poetry and fiction. She compared Chateaubriand's emotional, humane Christianity with the austere faith of Gerson in his *Imitation de Jésus Christ*, and gradually lost her vocation as a result. She found a kindred spirit in Rousseau with whose combination of true religious feeling and optimistic belief in humanity she felt totally in sympathy, and whose influence remained with her all her life. Sand avers that this was the time when she learned almost everything she now knows, and when she finally settled the question of her religious faith once and for all: 'Aussitôt que je me crus fondée à raisonner ma croyance et à l'épurer en lui cherchant l'appui et la sanction de mes meilleurs instincts, je n'eus plus de doute et je n'eus plus à revenir sur mes décisions' (I, 1089). As well as finding herself mentally and spiritually, the young girl also developed physically through her long, hard rides in the Berry countryside, and socially by her deliberate adoption of an eccentric lifestyle in defiance of local opinion. She compared herself to her male heroes, René, Byron, Hamlet and Alceste, and tried out one more possible end, that of suicide, but this also aborted thanks to the good sense of her horse, Colette, who kept going when Aurore half deliberately strayed into deep water while crossing the river Indre.

This interlude changed the young girl so dramatically that marriage could no longer provide a satisfactory ending to her story. In the *Histoire*, her engagement is quickly passed over, the ceremony is not described and the protagonist certainly did not live happily ever after. For a while, Aurore Dudevant tried to be a good wife and mother, sewing the layette for her first baby, Maurice, born nine months later; and here Sand briefly plays up her womanliness, praising and defending such female work. But she found this role impossible to sustain and quickly lapsed into illness and depression, suffering from 'une tristesse sans but et sans nom, maladive peut-être' (II, 47), which she tried to cure by constant travelling. Sand's description of these years, as we have seen, is vague and rapid, full of chronological in-accuracies, as though this time is a kind of blank in her mind, only briefly filled by more vivid memories of her stay in the Pyrenees and at her father-in-law's house at Guillery, although even here the essential (the Platonic affair with Aurélien de Sèze) is omitted; her passion for him is only referred to vaguely as 'quelque préoccupation intérieure' (II, 72) and he is merely 'un être absent' (II, 94). Everything seems bleak and oppressive, even the Berry countryside: 'Tout repose, mais tout semble mort' (II, 85), and the melancholy of the endless winters is only briefly alleviated by the somewhat forced gaiety of parties at La Châtre where she deliberatly outraged local opinion by ignoring accepted social distinctions. The death of Deschartres,[16] exiled in Paris, seems to encapsulate her sense of loss and despair at this time: 'Mais, en fait, il emportait avec lui dans le néant des choses finies toute une notable portion de ma vie, tous mes souvenirs d'enfance, agréables et tristes, tout le stimulant, tantôt fâcheux, tantôt bienfaisant, de mon développement intellectuel' (II, 55–6). Truly she seems to have lost her direction and to see no way out. And so the conventional ending is undermined, shown to be an impasse, and the ground is prepared for a new, alternative beginning.

Sand clearly makes of her departure to Paris in January 1831 a climax and a turning point. She not only begins another chapter but also renews her autobiographical pact with the reader, repeating the reasons for writing which she had given at the beginning of the book, once more setting her practice against that of Rousseau. This is the start of a new story, with a different protagonist, George Sand not Aurore Dupin/Dudevant. The past is finally liquidated. The cricket (symbol of hearth and home) who had been her companion in her little room at Nohant has died, and Sand sets up this death as symbolic of the end of all her hopes of domestic happiness: 'La mort du grillon marqua donc, comme d'une manière symbolique, la fin de mon séjour à Nohant' (II, 100). Then her arrival in Paris is marked by a series of farewells, to the convent which she visits for the last time, to her aristocratic friends, and to her mother-in-law who disowns her and

forbids her to use her married name.[17] Thus she makes clear as
narrator her entry into a different world. For the world she is now
entering is both classless and free, a man's world, the bohemian world
of the poor student, Rastignac or Frédéric Moreau, as the narrative at
this point rejoins the tradition of the *Bildungsroman*—after a series of
false starts and ten years later than if its protagonist had been a man.
Conforming to type, Aurore lived in a garret (although in the *Histoire*
it is with her daughter, not her lover, Sandeau, who is not
mentioned),[18] helping to create the cliché before it was a cliché:
'J'avais du ciel, de l'eau, de l'air, des hirondelles, de la verdure sur les
toits; je ne me sentais pas trop dans le Paris de la civilisation [...] mais
plutôt dans le Paris pittoresque et poétique de Victor Hugo, dans la
ville du passé' (II, 114). She wore men's clothes, delighting in the
comic misapprehensions which resulted; she frequented theatres and
cafés, fully aware that she was defying social convention, closing doors
so that others might open: 'Je choquais ouvertement la règle du
monde. Je me détachais de lui bien sciemment; je devais donc trouver
bon qu'il se détachât de moi dès qu'il saurait mes excentricités'
(II, 137).

The tone of this section of the autobiography is full of the
intoxication of self-discovery after depression and inertia.[19] In writing
of her decision to leave Nohant for Paris, Sand chooses to omit
various factors that were important in reality—an insulting letter she
found written for her by her husband, her desire to be with her new
lover—in order to highlight its fundamental significance, which had
less to do with her relations with others than with her relation to
herself. Hence the importance she attaches in the *Histoire* to her new
name, although not so much to the circumstances of its choice (as a
signature for *Indiana*) nor to the decision of what exactly it should be
(her editor, Delatouche, suggested Sand, a contraction of Sandeau
with whom she had written her first work, and she chose George 'vite
et sans chercher [...] qui me paraissait synonyme de Berrichon' (II,
138–9)). It is the new identity it denotes that she is proud to proclaim
to the world, 'une enseigne ou une devise' (II, 140), she calls it, the
result of a marriage between herself and the Muse. She is the name
and the name is her in a way that she never was the names she had
borne before. It brought with it no social or family baggage, no
constraints or expectations to limit her freedom: 'je l'ai fait moi-
même et moi seule après coup, par mon labeur' (II, 140). She still is
what she became then: 'aujourd'hui, comme il y a vingt ans, je vis, au-

jour le jour, de ce nom' (II, 140). She makes the substitution of one identity for another quite clear in a letter of 1832: '*A Paris Madame Dudevant est morte. Mais Georges Sand est connu pour un vigoureux gaillard.*'[20] The substitution here is crucially also one of gender, and is linked to her new environment; in Paris she is seen as a man, in Nohant she is still woman, wife and mother.

It is interesting that the assumption of the new identity which coincides with the new name takes precedence in the *Histoire* over the discovery of a vocation, since in reality of course Sand wrote *Indiana* before she needed to find a name with which to sign it. In describing and celebrating the identity first, she makes it clear that she came to Paris in order to find herself, not to be a writer. Her artistic vocation had been prefigured in her earlier account of a visit to the Louvre before her final departure for Paris, when she felt a new, higher world was revealed to her; and later she does give a sense of her destiny as a writer when she links the composition of *Indiana* to her childhood dreaming and particularly to her invention of Corambé. But her immediate concern at this crucial new beginning is with freedom and independence, not writing, so this is what comes first in the *Histoire*. She then has to backtrack in order to give an account of her apprenticeship as a young journalist working on the *Figaro* under Delatouche, and of her literary friendship with Balzac. She recounts an interview with the novelist Kératry who dismissed her literary ambitions with the summary advice: 'Croyez-moi [...] ne faites pas de livres, faites des enfants' (II, 150), altering for dramatic effect the true chronology by describing this meeting before the more sympathetic but less striking one with Delatouche, and comically highlighting the hostility she encountered as a woman. Although in a letter of 1831 she calls her newly found profession 'une passion',[21] in the *Histoire* she plays it down, says she began *Indiana* 'sans projet et sans espoir, sans aucun plan' (II, 160), mentioning only briefly 'une émotion très vive et très particulière' (II, 164) which the act of composition gave her; she maintains that she forgot her novels as soon as they were written and will not dwell on them in her autobiography. She does give an account of her theory of literary idealism, but retrospectively and set against Balzac's realism. This is probably, as we have already suggested, partly out of womanly modesty, but the defiant pride with which she had spoken of her new persona and new name suggests that she did not lack self-confidence and that writing was genuinely subordinate in her mind to her discovery of herself. Indeed we might well agree

that it is the personality behind the works that is exceptional rather
than the works themselves, particularly its play with gender, and this
was certainly the aspect that intrigued readers of *Indiana*, curious as to
who the mysterious G. Sand was: 'Les journaux parlèrent tous de
M. G. *Sand* avec éloge, insinuant que la main d'une femme avait dû
se glisser çà et là pour révéler à l'auteur certaines délicatesses du cœur
et de l'esprit, mais déclarant que le style et les appréciations avaient
trop de virilité pour n'être pas d'un homme' (II, 174).

The instant popular success of *Indiana* was followed seven months
later by the publication of *Valentine* in December 1832. In less than
two years Sand had arrived. The transformation was complete; from
now on she was George Sand to the public at large and soon to her
friends and family too. Her story could be thought to be at an end.
And yet, as the *Histoire* begins a new section, the tone abruptly
changes, the triumph turns into a defeat: her new, supposedly more
authentic persona became a burden as it brought with it public
responsibilities which took her over as completely as the private expectations of family had done before. She was never left alone, was
deluged by invitations and requests for help, so that the year 1833,
instead of being presented as the climax and resolution of her self-
construction, is described as beginning a new life of pain and forced
labour:

Cette année 1833 ouvrit pour moi la série des chagrins réels et profonds que
je croyais avoir épuisée et qui ne faisait que de commencer. J'avais voulu
être artiste, je l'étais enfin. Je m'imaginai être arrivée au but poursuivi
depuis longtemps, à l'indépendance extérieure et à la possession de ma
propre existence: je venais de river à mon pied une chaîne que je n'avais pas
prévue. (II, 181)

Her success as a writer, presented earlier as the fitting climax to a life
lived through the mind and the imagination, has now become a
destiny which is forced upon her. It is no longer a means of
transcending her womanhood but a prison into which that very
womanhood has locked her against her true nature, since it precluded
her from earning her living by any other means. She now denies that
she would have chosen a literary profession had there been any other
way, and dwells on the anguish and restlessness of these years 1833
to 1835, of which *Lélia* and the early *Lettres d'un voyageur* are an
expression. Thus again the shape of her narrative is qualified and
undercut. Of course, no *Bildungsroman* of any sophistication finishes

with a simple 'happy ever after'. Endings can be transcended (as in *Le Rouge et le noir*), left open (as in *Le Père Goriot*) or the whole tradition ironized (as in *L'Education sentimentale*). Of course too, an autobiography necessarily lacks the coherence and closure of fiction: again this is clear from Sand's predecessors and contemporaries. But the particular kind of reversal that we repeatedly find in Sand's *Histoire*, from triumph to defeat, pleasure to pain, independence to servitude, although partly the result of a Romantic malaise typical of her time, can surely also be attributed to the private self-doubts and public criticism to which a successful woman in the early nineteenth century was particularly prone, and which might lead her to underplay her achievements.

Sand's other strategy, conscious or unconscious, for making acceptable a persona and a vocation which were at odds with convention is rapidly to subordinate her own self-discovery to a quickened awareness of the existence of others, and in particular of their deprivation and pain, 'le mal général [...] la souffrance de la race entière' (II, 199). In this way, what had appeared to be the climax of her story becomes simply a stage in her development as her new realization of human misery leads away from an egoistic and unwomanly concern with self to a sense of solidarity with the people and her conversion to socialism. She even suggests in this context that the autobiography she is now writing is only the preface to a quite different book which will be concerned with politics and philosophy: 'Cet ouvrage-ci est la préface étendue et complète d'un livre qui paraîtra plus tard, et où, n'ayant plus à raconter ma propre histoire dans son développement minutieux et lent, je pourrai aborder des individualités plus importantes et plus intéressantes que la mienne propre' (II, 349). Suddenly, momentarily, our whole focus shifts; we are no longer reading the story of one woman's life for its intrinsic interest but as an introduction to reflection on public personalities and general issues. The individual disappears in favour of the universal, in keeping with Sand's justification, here taken to an extreme, that her life is only important for the lessons it can teach us all. Of course the other book was never written, the deferral remains suspended, and we are returned to our present narrative with an increased feeling of uncertainty as to what we are reading and why.

In the 1840s Sand was unusually politically active for a woman: in 1841 she set up the socialist *Revue indépendante* with Pierre Leroux, in 1844 she launched a republican paper in Orléans, *L'Eclaireur de l'Indre*, and in 1848 she acted briefly as unofficial Minister of Propaganda for the new Republican government. None of this is mentioned in the *Histoire*. She attributes her initial conversion to politics to Michel de Bourges (Everard in the *Histoire*), although she reserved the right to disagree with him on certain questions, refusing to abandon completely her 'feminine' way of thinking (as he saw it). She also describes at length the ideas and personalities of Lamennais and Leroux and their influence on her. It is true that she was not an original thinker, that her version of Utopian socialism is highly derivative of Leroux in particular, but she was certainly more active and strong-minded than she makes herself appear in her auto-biography where her account of her politicization is often undercut by modest disclaimers as to her own capacities.

Her development from individualism to socialism is not presented as continuous or straightforward. In the *Histoire* (as no doubt in her life) it is constantly interrupted by an account of her personal battle for a legal separation from her husband and for repossession of Nohant. The two processes are narrated in parallel and correspond to the two sides of Sand's personality, the public and the private, linked to the two opposing environments, Paris and Nohant, between which she shuttled all her life. Although she frequently spent periods of some months at Nohant in the years 1831 to 1835, she says she felt less and less at home there—'Mes enfants ni ma maison ne m'appartenaient, moralement parlant' (II, 293)—and increasingly rootless: 'Je n'étais bien nulle part' (II, 308). She does not describe the actual scene which triggered her demand for a separation—when Casimir threatened her with a gun in the course of a family quarrel—obviously out of discretion but also because a far more fundamental reason was her pressing need to reintegrate her roots, win back her children and strengthen the thread which led from her own childhood to theirs and also to her future grandchildren. For Nohant represented a continuity and stability which was as essential to her as her active literary and political life in Paris. She emphasizes the link between the generations from her vantage point in 1855 in her description of a final family picnic before the beginning of the separation proceedings during which she was banned from Nohant (although for less long than she suggests in the *Histoire*). She is speaking of her grand-daughter who had recently died: 'vingt ans plus tard, j'ai eu à mes côtés un autre enfant rayonnant de force, de bonheur et de beauté, bondissant sur la mousse des bois et la ramassant dans les plis de sa robe comme avait fait sa mère, comme j'avais fait moi-même, dans les mêmes lieux, dans les mêmes jeux, dans les mêmes rêves d'or et de fées' (II, 369). Her reintegration of Nohant was essential to the completion of her story, for only there could her quest and conversion plot be consummated by a return, the new self join up with the old and she be complete. Here too Sand follows the pattern of traditional autobiographies (by St Augustine or Rousseau, for example) which end with a similar need to return to childhood origins, but Sand embeds her own return more firmly within a family line.

In 1836, after a year of litigation and constant travelling—'une année de luttes amères' (II, 387)—Sand finally won her case against her husband. In the *Histoire*, she joyfully celebrates her triumphal re-entry into Nohant as its sole owner and as guardian of Solange (guardianship of Maurice was to come later): 'Je partis pour Nohant, où je rentrai définitivement avec Solange le jour de Sainte-Anne, patronne du village. On dansait sous les grands ormes, et le son rauque et criard de la cornemuse, si cher aux oreilles qu'il a bercées dès l'enfance, eût pu me paraître d'un heureux augure' (II, 388). Once again, though, already hinted at here, the victory turns sour, as Sand begins the next chapter by emphasizing not the pleasures of her new life but its problems and pain: 'Je n'avais pourtant pas conquis la moindre aisance' (II, 389). She recognizes that she brings with her wherever she goes her difficult inheritance and conflicting needs. By triumphing over her woman's fate, she says, she only increased her burden, thus paradoxically turning her success as an independent woman into a plea for the sanctity of marriage, albeit a marriage between equals. Here theory and practice seem curiously at odds, and the message of the life is contradictory. Happiness is impossible for a woman; whichever path she chooses, domesticity or a public career, she is doomed to dissatisfaction and a sense of loss. Nohant, however, remains crucial to something more profound than happiness, to Sand's very sense of her own identity. Her family home is an example of 'ces demeures pleines d'images douces et cruelles, histoire de votre propre vie, écrite sur tous les murs en caractères mystérieux et indélébiles, qui, à chaque ébranlement de l'âme, vous entourent d'émotions profondes ou de puériles superstitions' (II, 389). The actual building has become a text, the story of a destiny like the one we are reading, as confused and ambiguous, but enriched by associations with the past and anticipations of the future and therefore an essential doubling of the written autobiography, its embodiment in stone.

Not that Sand stayed there for long. The narrative moves on quickly to bring us up to date, giving a brief account of her travels in Switzerland with Marie d'Agoult and Liszt (already described in the *Entretiens journaliers avec le très docte et très habile docteur Piffoël* and the tenth *Lettre d'un voyageur*), then of her busy literary and political life in Paris, the death of her mother and disintegrating relationship with Everard whose death in 1853 she anticipates. This acts as a transition to her first mention of Chopin which introduces the final section of the *Histoire* and brings us rapidly up to the time of writing. During these last years, she lived a chaste, domestic life with Chopin and her children, in Paris during the winter and at Nohant in the summer, 'la vie de famille et d'intérieur me devenant chaque jour plus chère et plus nécessaire' (II, 436). She is apparently finally happy, more tolerant and less demanding than before, living for love, but again her serenity is presented as veiling an inner melancholy and even despair which is largely unexplained but could be the result of particular misfortunes which she does not specify (perhaps because they were too close to be confronted directly): we know of the rift with Solange and Chopin in 1847, his death in 1849 and the death of her granddaughter in 1855. Thus the conclusion of this exemplary *Bildungsroman*, this story of an extraordinary woman who might be said to have succeeded in every sphere, is marked by a terrible sense of loss, a deep pessimism not only about her own life but also for her century which she thinks has lost its way. This is partly mitigated by a vague faith in immortality, and a reiteration of the salutary effect of her message of suffering for us all, but the overall tone is profoundly sad. By definition an autobiography can have no obvious end, and some purposefully look forward rather than back in their closing pages. Sand's *Histoire de ma vie*, however, does come to a despairing conclusion with a kind of peroration, whose content has more in common with Simone de Beauvoir's 'je mesure avec stupeur à quel point j'ai été flouée'[22] than with the apparent confidence of the last words of Sartre's *Les Mots*: 'que reste-t-il? Tout un homme, fait de tous les hommes et qui les vaut tous et que vaut n'importe qui.'[23] The last person Sand recalls, on the closing page, is Marie Dorval; it is her woman's story that acts as a final reference point and the text ends with a cry of solidarity with her friend whom the world had destroyed and who died of grief: 'Marie Dorval est morte de sa douleur, et moi, j'ai pu rester debout, hélas!' (II, 461).

There is no doubt that the structure of the *Histoire*, as we look back over it from the perspective of its end, gives us a strong sense of the growth of a self within time and the achievement of an identity (however complex). We may, however, be equally struck by the pattern of oscillation which disturbs the progressive forward movement as the self cannot be contained within any simple linear scheme. Although Roy Pascal maintains that such a structural feature can be found in many autobiographies,[24] it is more usually associated with texts by women, and may be connected to their relationship with their mothers from whom separation is more difficult. Elizabeth Abel speaks of 'the fluctuations of symbiosis and separation from the mother'[25] which characterize women's lives and Freud had earlier linked such fluctuations to alternative gender identifications in a way which is particularly relevant to Sand: 'Regressions to the fixations of the pre-Oedipus phases very frequently occur; in the course of some women's lives there is a repeated alternation between periods in which masculinity or femininity gains the upper hand';[26] thus the Oedipal crisis is prolonged for years into adulthood. We may not agree with too narrowly Freudian an interpretation but the structure of oscillation in women's autobiographies, and in Sand's *Histoire de ma vie*, can equally well be seen in more general terms, as expressive of a woman's different life experience marked more obviously by opposition and conflict—between the private and the public, the self and other, inner and outer—making each achievement more precarious and coherence more difficult to achieve.

Sand sees such oppositions as fundamental to her identity and also recognizes the part they played in patterning her life: 'Quant à moi, je me retrouvais .dans une des deux faces de mon caractère, tout comme à Nohant de huit à douze ans, tout comme au couvent de treize à seize, alternative continuelle de solitude recueillie et d'étourdissement complet' (II, 40). It is no surprise, then, to see the plot of her life's text in similar terms, as each step in one direction is followed by regression or reversal. The process could be said to have started with her father's death which cut short the normal development of the little girl, fixing her for much longer, one might say, in the pre-Oedipal stage. As a result perhaps of the insecurity this bred in her as well as of conflicting public expectations, the triumphant tone with which she describes each of her achievements is often, as we have seen, negated by an emphasis on the suffering to which it led, sufferings which were both mental and physical (and illness is a recurrent theme in women's texts, often seen as an expression of the author's rejection of her female body). Alternatively, the playing out of one identity is followed by a swing to the other extreme as opposing influences and needs turn out to be equally pressing and incompatible. So a pattern of oscillation is set up: from being a 'diable' she became a 'saint', the fulfilment of childbirth turned into chronic depression, the publication of *Indiana* was followed by a need for solitude which led to a conversion to socialism, and immediately after her final repossession of Nohant Sand left for Switzerland and Paris.

Certain theorists also suggest that turning points are presented differently in women's autobiographies, as sudden awakenings, flashes of intuition rather than reasoned decisions: 'Men tend to move on a fairly predictable path to achievement; women transform themselves only after an awakening.'[27] One would of course expect religious conversions to be described in this way, and Sand certainly stresses that her moment of revelation and conversion in the church at the convent took her completely unawares, although she now understands how prepared she was for it psychologically. She does not see it, though, as a truly spiritual experience but as the young girl's emotional and imaginative response to the sensuous atmosphere in the church that evening, when the darkness was lit up by the reflection of candlelight in the polished marble floor and in the gold of the picture frames and the altar, just as earlier her eye had been drawn to the warm colours of Titian's painting of *The Agony in the Garden* also in the convent church. The scent of honeysuckle and jasmine drifts in from the garden, a star shines through the window and the birds are singing:

c'était un calme, un charme, un recueillement, un mystère, dont je n'avais jamais eu l'idée […]. Je ne sais ce qui se passait en moi. Je respirais une atmosphère d'une suavité indicible, et je la respirais par l'âme plus encore que par les sens. Tout à coup je ne sais quel ébranlement se produisit dans tout mon être, un vertige passe devant mes yeux comme une lueur blanche dont je me sens enveloppée. Je crois entendre une voix murmurer à mon oreille: *Tolle, lege.* (I, 953–4)

Since Sand denies that this sudden illumination was a miracle, it is easier to make the connection with other clearly secular moments which she describes in the same way, as quasi-religious conversions. Thus the revelation of her vocation as an artist also came upon her unexpectedly, out of the blue, not as a result of her experiments in the craft of writing but displaced back to a routine visit to the Louvre in June 1830. She claims to have known nothing about art, but her intuitive response to the paintings was overwhelming, evidently reminiscent of the effect the Titian canvas had had on her in the convent church. She feels transported into another world: 'Il me semblait avoir conquis je ne sais quel trésor d'infini dont j'avais ignoré l'existence. Je n'aurais pu dire quoi, je ne savais pas de nom pour ce que je sentais se presser dans mon esprit réchauffé et comme dilaté; mais j'avais la fièvre, et je m'en revenais du musée, me perdant de rue en rue, ne sachant où j'allais, oubliant de manger' (II, 107). Two pages later, she leaves for Paris, and this passage clearly serves as a prefiguration of the new world of art and literature which she is entering and in which she will feel so at home. Five years on, her first political discussion with Everard is similarly described. He appears to her transfigured, like a divinity, and his words have an all-embracing and uplifting effect; she herself calls the change in her a conversion. The fact that she clearly fell in love with him that night as well as becoming a socialist simply reinforces the conclusion that we can draw from all these experiences, that the transformations that took place in Sand almost always appear as the result of emotional stimulation rather than rational deliberation, and so fit in with the different way a woman is said to determine her destiny.

There is one final feature of the structure of the *Histoire* whose oddness is striking and which can also perhaps be explained in terms of the specificity of a woman's text. At two key inaugural points, when relating her birth and her birth to writing, Sand seems to have great difficulty in getting her story going, in disentangling it from the stories of others. Béatrice Didier attributes this to the scandals associated with both moments,[28] but the inhibition is perhaps more fundamental and linked to Sand's female identity. She first announces her birth as a historical fact on page 13, but goes on to devote the next 400 pages to an account of her antecedents. Her birth is then restated still as part of her father's story, at the end of a long sentence, almost as an afterthought. It next appears casually some forty pages later in the context of her mother's life as well as of her father's deception of her grandmother, and she gets the date wrong:[29] 'Cet accident de quitter le sein de ma mère m'arriva à Paris le 16 messidor an XII' (I, 461). The fourth reference gives a more detailed account of the happy circumstances of the birth (with the right date this time), repeated again a few pages later on: 'Le 5 juillet 1804 je vins au monde, mon père jouant du violon et ma mère ayant une jolie robe rose' (I, 466); now both parents are equally important. Sand then tells us how it was only when doing the research for her autobiography that she was able to establish who she really was; before this, she says, she was rumoured to have been born one or two years earlier in Madrid, and therefore not to be the person named on her birth certificate. Only now can she be sure of her identity and state definitely (and for the sixth time): 'Je suis bien née à Paris le 5 juillet 1804, je suis bien *moi-même* en un mot' (I, 468). Thus her autobiographical project brought literal self-knowledge, focused on the actual moment of her arrival in the world, although the importance of this discovery for the adult Sand may seem to us strangely underplayed. There is one last mention of the birth before the narrative is finally launched into a description of the early years in Paris. What can we make of this stuttering opening? Why does Sand feel the need to state no less than six times that she was born? Does the reiteration in different contexts and from different points of view reinforce the reader's sense of her beginning or play it down? We might see it as a kind of female self-deprecation which refuses to set up her own birth as dramatically and self-evidently important but embeds it in a public and familial environment in order to make it clear that her life is also a narrative of her time. Or perhaps it is simply the result of a certain loquacity, a carelessness in the structuring of the text. However we explain it, we cannot but find it significant, revealing of the uncertainty of Sand's attitude to both her life and her autobiography, as she seems in two minds as to how to get started.

Sand's decision to leave Nohant for Paris, her birth to herself, is similarly oddly presented although for different and perhaps more understandable reasons. For here she is clearly going against traditional expectations, so that rather than subordinating her story to that of others she needs to bring it into relief, to explain and justify the new turn it is taking. Again her first mention of the decision is rapid and matter-of-fact, at the end of a quick overview of the years 1826 to 1831, as though it were an event like any other for which she gives the briefest and vaguest of motivations: 'A partir de ce moment-là, l'équilibre entre les peines et les satisfactions se trouva rompu. Je sentis la nécessité de prendre un parti. Je le pris sans hésiter, et mon mari y donna les mains: j'allai vivre à Paris avec ma fille, moyennant un arrangement qui me permettait de revenir tous les trois mois passer trois mois à Nohant' (II, 91). She then finds it necessary to backtrack, to give a context to this unorthodox move and lead back into it from other directions. First, she justifies her departure by giving a lengthy account of her state of mind during the preceding four years, stressing her loneliness and frustrated idealism, and seeing herself as a victim of her situation. Then she takes a different tack, recapitulating the whole story of her marriage in order to emphasize her financial dependence on her husband and the vain practical steps she took to remedy the situation. These two aspects of her dissatisfaction, her idealism and her need for independence, come together in what appears as the crucial immediate trigger to her departure—that visit to the Louvre which was to lead indirectly to her decision to be a writer. The tone all through these pages is both tentative and challenging, and demonstrates clearly Sand's awareness that here her life is in complete defiance of convention. Her odd presentation of this, the climax of her *Bildungsroman*, is thus exemplary of the unease she felt, no doubt unconsciously, within the male tradition which was her only model. For ultimately, of course, Sand's experience was that of a woman, not a man; and just as the little girl's passionate adoration of her mother pierces through the neutrally objective account of her childhood, so the young woman's anxiety about the taboos she was breaking in her life surfaces at key moments to disturb the basic linear structure of the text.

Notes to Chapter 3

1. Paul John Eakin, 'Narrative and chronology as structures of reference and the new model autobiographer', in *Studies in Autobiography*, ed. James Olney (Oxford: Oxford University Press, 1988), 39.
2. Coe, *When the Grass was Taller*, 169.
3. Lejeune, *L'Autobiographie en France*, 14.
4. Patricia Spacks, *Imagining a Self: Autobiography and the Novel in Eighteenth Century England* (Cambridge, Mass.: Harvard University Press, 1976), 10.
5. Pascal, *Design and Truth in Autobiography*, 112.
6. Julia Watson, 'Shadowed Presence: Women's Autobiographies and the Other', in *Studies in Autobiography*, ed. Olney, 183.
7. Sheringham, *French Autobiography*, 103.
8. Burton Pike, 'Time in autobiography', *Comparative Literature* 28 (1976), 334.
9. Sand, *Correspondance*, viii. 188.
10. See Rachel Blau du Plessis, *Writing beyond the Ending* (Bloomington: Indiana University Press, 1985), 1.
11. Elizabeth Abel, Marianne Hirsch and Elizabeth Langland (eds.), *The Voyage In: Fictions of Female Development* (Hanover and London: University Press of New England, 1983), 11.
12. Frappier-Mazur, 'Nostalgie, dédoublement et écriture', 269.

13. Bozon-Scalzetti, 'Vérité de la fiction', 103.
14. Frappier-Mazur, 'Nostalgie, dédoublement et écriture', 269.
15. Susan Sellers, *Language and Sexual Difference: Feminist Writing in France* (London: Macmillan, 1991), 50.
16. Deschartres died in 1828 but in the *Histoire* Sand brings his death forward to 1825.
17. This effectively precluded Sand from using the customary Madame de ... as her professional name and forced her to find a pseudonym.
18. In reality, Sand only brought Solange with her to Paris the following year.
19. The letters written at this time are more sober, and emphasize more Sand's regret for the children she left behind.
20. Sand, *Correspondance*, ii. 120.
21. Sand, *Correspondance*, i. 813.
22. Simone de Beauvoir, *La Force des choses* (Paris: Gallimard, 1963), ii. 508.
23. Jean-Paul Sartre, *Les Mots* (Paris: Gallimard, 1964), 213.
24. Pascal, *Design and Truth in Autobiography*, 17.
25. Abel, Hirsch and Langland (eds.), *The Voyage In*, 10.
26. Freud, 'Femininity', 429.
27. Carolyn G. Heilbrun, *Writing a Woman's Life* (London: Woman's Press, 1989), 118. See also Abel, Hirsch and Langland (eds.), *The Voyage In*, 12.
28. Béatrice Didier, 'Femme, identité, écriture', 562.
29. Perhaps this is because she is here using the Revolutionary calendar.

CHAPTER 4

Identity and Writing

The identity constructed by an autobiography is necessarily double, composed of a young protagonist and a narrating voice whose presence is much more strongly felt than in fiction. Moreover, neither of these identities is fixed, since both exist and evolve within time, whether it be the time of the life within the text or the time of narration outside it. Some autobiographers ignore this second temporal level and write about their younger selves as though from some fixed point outside time like the extra-diagetic narrator in a novel, but others, and Sand is one of them, give us a strong sense of a double movement forward, of two selves advancing in parallel. At first the gap between them is obvious and wide, but it gradually closes as the text proceeds, as the younger self draws nearer to the adult voice, although the two can never entirely merge; for it is impossible to be both subject and object simultaneously, the writing self will always be one step ahead of the self being written about, and is itself subject to further change. An autobiographical text, then, is never completely closed, unified and self-contained. The identity it projects will always be elusive, coinciding neither with itself nor with the living person who wrote it, leaving gaps that cannot be filled, openings for interpretation. As Sheringham puts it: 'The subject of autobiography is a hybrid, a fusion of past and present, self and other, document and desire, referential and textual, *énoncé* and *énonciation*— not a product but a process.'[1]

The immediate focus of the text for the reader is bound to be the younger self, for it is his/her story that is being told, and much of the work of interpretation here has already been done by the adult narrator. She has had to reinvent herself from the outside, transform herself for public consumption into an object containable and explicable in words (at least in a traditional autobiography, influenced by positivist cultural models of identity and narrative). Thus the *Histoire*

de ma vie is punctuated by generalizing descriptions which make sense
of the feelings and behaviour of the protagonist in terms of certain
ordering schemes and recognizable human types. Sand is anxious to
deny any over-simplification in her self-presentation but frequently
resorts to a rhetoric of dualities and oppositions to clarify and make
familiar her own 'étoffe [...] bigarrée' (II, 160). These she attributes
both to the important influences on her (mother/grandmother,
Paris/Nohant, Chateaubriand/Gerson), and to her own temperament. Most often the contrast is between frenetic activity and intense
solitary contemplation: 'Mon corps et mon esprit se commandaient
alternativement une inquiétude d'activité et une fièvre de con-
templations' (I, 823), and later readers of Sand have often agreed with
her own self-construction. Henry James, for example, describes her as
a 'singular mixture of quietude and turbulence',[2] and Ruth Jordan
defines her entirely in terms of oppositions: 'a person of many facets,
ambitious as well as self-deprecating, generous as well as mean, selfless
as well as selfish, idealistic as well as practical'.[3] (We might also refer
back to the structure of alternation and oscillation discussed in
Chapter 3.) It is difficult, however, not to feel that by inscribing her
within such pre-established structural and linguistic patterns these
polarizations belie to some degree the complexity of the living
person.[4]

It may be more revealing to look at the narrating voice, George
Sand, as she constructs herself in the present moment of writing,
rather than the young Aurore Dupin of whom we are given a more
controlled picture because it is retrospective. It is, of course, the very
writing of the autobiography that makes the link between the two,
that completes the process of transformation from the one into the
other by spelling it out, thus giving the name George Sand a lineage
and a context, a kind of guarantee. Sand is no longer trying to disown
her past as she was at the age of 26 on her move to Paris, but to
reclaim it, recognizing now that she could never have become George
Sand had she not been Aurore Dupin first. The new identity,
however, is clearly the important one, and particularly so because it
no longer confines its owner within one gender and one role. By
changing her name, Sand carried through 'her own beheading' of
father and husband, as Anne Freadman puts it,[5] and went on alone to
found a new line, bearing a new name which nobody had borne
before. She describes its taking on as though it were a marriage
between the man and the woman in her: 'un contrat, un nouveau

mariage entre le pauvre apprenti poète que j'étais et l'humble muse qui m'avait consolée dans mes peines' (II, 140). Since she quickly dropped the *s* from Georges, the name was truly hermaphroditic (a man's name ending with a feminine *e*), although she soon became known also as Madame Sand as others attempted to pigeonhole her back into a recognizable social position. She disliked this form of address, however, signed her letters 'George' (or did not sign them at all) and made her preference for the masculine identity quite clear in a letter of 1836: 'Madame Sand est une bête que je ne vous engage pas à connaître et qui vous ennuierait mortellement; mais George est un excellent garçon, plein de cœur et de reconnaissance pour ceux qui veulent bien l'aimer.'[6]

As well as detaching her from any normal categorization by gender, this invented name which appeared out of nowhere (the link with Sandeau quickly became irrelevant) also removed her from any clear affiliation to social class. By first living the bohemian life of a young student and then surrounding herself with an eclectic group of artists, poets and thinkers as well as the workers and artisans she befriended in the 1840s, Sand effectively created her own space, 'un lieu symbolique, hors sexe et hors société, qui permet d'être ailleurs', as Nicole Mozet puts it.[7] Her actual home, the place she made her own, was of course Nohant. Nohant is Mozet's 'ailleurs', in so far as the symbolic, inner space of which Mozet is speaking can ever be actualized, and it is true that the social and literary life Sand lived there, the odd family structures which it contained, were eccentric, unique. Nohant itself, though, the house and the estate, were embedded in history and provided her with roots which gave her the stability and self-confidence to carry through her transformation and then to write about it. She was not writing from nowhere, from some abstract place out of time and out of the world, but from a perspective clearly situated within contemporary history and from a position of respectability and even authority: freed from social and gender constraints, perhaps, but not unaware of them, able to negotiate them with flexibility and inventiveness.

Indeed, as narrator of the *Histoire* Sand was very clearly writing within the context of her time, as the events of 1848 interrupted its composition for a few months and altered her perspective on her story. When she picked up her pen again, she noted the change in herself: 'J'ai beaucoup appris, beaucoup vécu, beaucoup vieilli durant ce court intervalle [...]. Si j'eusse fini mon livre avant cette révolution, c'eût été un autre livre' (I, 465). She has lost her illusions, she says, disappointed by the outcome of the February revolution in which she had placed such high hopes. Yet she understands that her present pessimism is not definitive, that she may change again: 'Mon livre sera donc triste si je reste sous l'impression que j'ai reçue dans ces derniers temps. Mais qui sait? le temps marche vite' (I, 465). Sand shows an unusual awareness of the historicity of her narrative, its provisional quality. It took her a leisurely seven years to write it and she lived and changed along with it. Her mood varies, affected by the acts of remembering and writing down the past as well as affecting them. Sometimes she feels able to stand outside her life and view it *sub specie aeternitatis*, 'avec le même calme et le même esprit de justice que si j'étais, avec la pleine possession de ma lucidité, *in articulo mortis*' (II, 289). Elsewhere she is so moved by her memories that she can hardly put pen to paper: 'j'ai peine à écrire en cet instant, et le souvenir de ce triple passé sans lendemain m'oppresse et m'étouffe' (II, 370). She knows too that time cannot be arrested, that her own text exists within it and that her future readers' perspectives may be different from hers: 'ce présent, le moment où l'on écrit, c'est déjà le passé pour ceux qui vous lisent au bout de quelques années. L'écrivain a quelquefois aussi envisagé l'avenir. Ses prédictions se trouvent déjà réalisées ou démenties quand son œuvre paraît' (I, 156). No definitive view is possible; all we can do is remain open to the changing course of history, our own and that of others.

It is of course unwise to suggest that this enlightened, contemplative narrative voice coincides totally with the real woman. The link is closer in autobiography than in a novel like *La Vie de Marianne* or *Jane Eyre*, but a real person exists separately from reflection and language, in a physical world of being. The assumption of a voice presupposes a choice, conscious or unconscious, of a certain style and register, also conditioned by generic and linguistic conventions of the time. A certain level of intentionality is at work which places a gap between the original self and the text. Moreover, the identity created by an autobiography only exists and acquires substance through language, and language also has a momentum of its own; thus the George Sand who speaks in the *Histoire* is partly a literary construction, different from the living person who wrote it. This is borne out by the very different voices Sand adopts in her other autobiographical writings; in the twelve *Lettres d'un voyageur* in particular, as we have seen, she uses a number of rhetorical strategies, writes in diverse tones and styles, to create a series of different selves at will. Through writing, the autobiographer 'enhances his condition, extends himself beyond his unwritten self',[8] and here the extension goes in many directions, to explore the potential for self-creation and transformation of the young Sand of the 1830s. By the time she wrote the *Histoire*, she needed to project a more stable, authoritative and reflective image, the image of somebody who has lived much and has learned from experience, so she addressed the reader in a less playful tone, not so obviously self-conscious but with an element of deliberation all the same.

Certain contemporary feminist theorists have spoken of a kind of writing (to which Hélène Cixous has given the name 'écriture féminine') whose distinctiveness would lie in its escape from the artificially ordering structures of 'patriarchal' language. Although Cixous does not deny men the possibility of such a subversive writing practice, citing Genet, Kleist and James Joyce, for example, she argues that it has a greater relevance for women, since they have long felt less at home in conventional language than men. The idea of a woman's different experience producing a 'woman's sentence' goes back to Virginia Woolf who defined it thus: 'She had a sensibility that was very wide, eager and free. It responded to an almost imperceptible touch on it [...]. It ranged too, very subtly and curiously, among almost unknown or unrecorded things; it lighted on small things and showed that perhaps they were not small after all. It brought buried things to light.'[9] Women have the potential to escape from the confines of systems and hierarchies, to write in a different way and of what has never been written about before. For Woolf, however, the ideal language would be androgynous, embracing the strengths of both men and women, be as she puts it 'woman-manly or man-womanly',[10] and it is impossible not to think of Sand here although she may not have the stature of the androgynous writers Woolf admires most, Shakespeare, Coleridge and Proust.

Woolf's feminism, however, is considerably less aggressive than that of the French feminists of the 1970s and 80s. There is a certain polemic violence in their call to women to speak out of the silence that has stifled them for centuries, to speak in their own language which has so far been repressed by a phallocentric order (although the political inference could also be seen as a strategy to encourage freer and more diverse writing practices among men as well as women). 'Ecris-toi,' urges Cixous in *Le Rire de la Méduse*, 'il faut que ton corps se fasse entendre. Alors jailliront les immenses ressources de l'inconscient. [...] Ecrire, acte qui non seulement "réalisera" le rapport dé-censuré de la femme à sa sexualité, à son être-femme, lui rendant accès à ses propres forces; qui lui rendra ses biens, ses plaisirs, ses organes, ses immenses territoires corporels tenus sous scellés.'[11] A woman must write with her body, constantly recreating the body through writing, in order to recapture that oneness with her mother and herself which she lost when she entered the masculine world of the Law. Because of her capacity to give birth, a woman is more in tune with the rhythms of her body and it is these that should inform her writing practice. She must also be open to other voices speaking from the unconscious and from elsewhere, so that her language is not linear and unified but brimming with a profusion of possible meanings, always open to revision, defying order and rationality through allusion, repetition, fragmentation and metaphor.

Luce Irigaray uses similarly physical imagery, making it more explicitly sexual when she associates woman's discourse with the plurality of female genitalia to argue for a language which speaks of woman's desire as subject as well as object.[12] Julia Kristeva's notion of the 'semiotic' also has a certain affinity with Cixous's privileging of early childhood and the mother figure, both corresponding in some ways to Freud's pre-Oedipal stage and Lacan's Imaginary within which the child (boy and girl) dwells before its necessary move into the 'symbolic' language of the father, although Kristeva does not particularly associate the 'semiotic' with writing by women. The 'semiotic chora' (or womb), as she calls it in *La Révolution du langage poétique*, expresses the basic energy drives of the physical: 'Il s'agit donc de fonctions sémiotiques pré-œdipiennes, de décharges d'énergie qui lient et orientent le corps par rapport à la mère.'[13] It is not strictly a language but corresponds perhaps to the babbling of babies, to rhythm and intonation, and survives to disrupt the ordered structures of conventional writing.

In *Bearing the Word*, the American critic, Margaret Homans, places a rather different emphasis. For her, what distinguishes a feminine from a masculine discourse (and she is speaking of actual writers such as Dorothy Wordsworth, the Brontës, as well as Woolf, in their relation to the real world) is a preference for the literal over the figurative. By literal she means 'a lack of gap between signifier and referent',[14] so that words come as close as possible to the thing they name, an attempt at coincidence with the object, the physical world, which is reminiscent of Cixous's ideal of a coincidence between language and the subject writer's physical body. Homans also has in common with Kristeva the notion of a duality within certain forms of writing: a woman retains the possibility of using two kinds of discourse, the literal and the figurative, so that in the same way as for Kristeva the 'semiotic' remains within the 'symbolic' to subvert it, so literal writing can co-exist with the figurative. Otherwise Homans's identification of the feminine with the literal would deny women the use of metaphor, and also the practice of irony which demands by definition that a text should not be read literally.

What is the relevance of such modernist speculation to the writings of Sand who lived 150 years earlier? By taking on a male pseudonym, she was seeking to avoid being read as a woman precisely in order to escape confinement within a female stereotype, and also because a 'feminine' style was considered inferior. Moreover, as we have seen, 'écriture féminine' can be written by men (so it might be equally appropriate to study Flaubert or any other male writer from this perspective), or it may only exist as a potential. One could also argue that if it does exist, it is as artificial and studied a style as any other, the brainchild of the self-conscious literary theorizing of the late twentieth century, and that writing can never be completely unmediated (as indeed such theorists recognize). Yet although there is no question of there having been a particular kind of discourse associated with women in the early nineteenth century, Sand's style was described as 'feminine' by many, as though she could not help writing as she did because she was a woman; and the terms used do correspond in certain ways to the specificity of female writing as seen by modern feminists. I would not wish to conclude that there is something essentially and ahistorically different about the way women write. However, it may be revealing to see how Sand has been thus categorized, and then to point out the many diverse features of the language of her autobiography; whether direct ('female') or deliberately chosen ('male'), they work together to communicate an identity whose plurality goes beyond both gender stereotypes.

To begin with, it is striking how often her writing has been associated with various bodily functions, as though it were a physical as much as a mental activity, reminding us of Cixous's call to women to write their bodies.[15] Sand herself, in a letter to Flaubert, compares it to weeping in order both to stress its instinctive spontaneity as opposed to Flaubert's highly self-conscious style, and to point out the total coincidence she felt between the woman she was and her narrating voice: 'ne pas se donner tout entier dans son œuvre, me paraît aussi impossible que de pleurer avec autre chose que ses yeux'[16] (although the generalizing masculine gender she uses suggests she does not see this characteristic as peculiar to women). Some of her male colleagues describe her writing in the same way, although the vulgar imagery they use makes quite clear what they see as her womanly inferiority. Thus Proudhon wrote of her: 'Cette femme écrit comme elle pisse',[17] Jules Renard called her 'la vache bretonne de la littérature',[18] and Baudelaire compared her with a 'latrine' in the most offensively scatological insult of them all.[19] A few years earlier, however, he had been less abusive, mocking the uncontrolled verbosity of all women and only reluctantly including Sand:

Les femmes écrivent, écrivent avec une rapidité débordante; leur cœur bavarde à la rame. Elles ne connaissent généralement ni l'art, ni la mesure, ni la logique; leur style traîne et ondoie comme leurs vêtements. Un très grand et très justement illustre écrivain, George Sand elle-même, n'a pas tout à fait, malgré sa supériorité, échappé à cette loi du tempérament; elle jette ses chefs-d'œuvre à la poste comme des lettres.[20]

Henry James agrees but uses more flattering terms, praising her imagination 'almost of the first order' and her 'gift of speech, speech supreme and inspired',[21] while still identifying her wordiness with her womanhood: 'She has all a woman's loquacity, but she has never a woman's shrillness.'[22] Artlessness, a natural facility with words, have long been seen as the special gift of women and may be admired as well as abused. Baudelaire in even softer mood is responsive to the peculiarly feminine charm of the poetry of Marceline Desbordes-Valmore, its simple and sincere expression of the author's fears, joys and desires.[23] Women are generally thought to be more attuned to the subtle movements of the heart, able to express feeling more directly, without self-consciousness. *Indiana* was discussed by contemporaries in precisely these stereotypical terms: 'Après avoir lu et relu, *on demeure confondu d'étonnement quand on songe qu'une femme en est l'auteur*, une femme délicate et frêle proie du don admirable d'écrire, qu'une simple femme, ayant des larmes dans la voix et dans le cœur, on le sent bien, a su jeter ce regard ferme sur la société.'[24]

In the *Histoire*, Sand links her gift of speech intimately with her mother, reminding us again of Cixous and Kristeva. In her earliest years, her mother sang to her, read to her, told her stories, and through the security provided by her constant presence encouraged the child into the world of language in which she revelled without embarrassment or inhibition. When later her mother left her, she instinctively retreated into the same world of the imagination in order to make up for her absence: 'quand j'avais du chagrin, quand je pensais à ma petite mère absente, c'étaient des complaintes en mineur qui ne finissaient pas et qui endormaient peu à peu ma mélancolie ou qui provoquaient des larmes dont j'étais soulagée' (I, 805–6), until eventually Corambé appeared to fill the void. The stories which flowed in her head like water from a fountain[25] had no structure and little coherence, continuing interminably from day to day without ever coming to an end, reminding Sand and the reader of the facility and regularity—'un laisser-aller invincible' (I, 542)—with which she was to write her novels all her life. She maintained that for her writing was an activity like any other, like gardening or sewing: 'J'y suis tellement habituée à présent que j'écris avec autant de facilité que je ferais un ourlet.'[26] It was part of her domestic routine, not specially privileged or set apart: 'Toute ma vie j'avais eu un roman en train dans la cervelle' (I, 808), just as her pseudonym quickly came to signify the whole person, not simply the professional writer. In a strange way, then, perhaps out of a feminine modesty which is partly genuine and partly assumed, she appears to agree with Proudhon and Baudelaire in defining writing as a natural activity which she can perform almost without conscious thought, although the terms she uses are considerably less vulgar and debasing.[27]

Long before the emergence, then, of contemporary feminist theory, writers and readers have felt that there was something different about women's language, specifying features that many women have in common and few men—and have included Sand. But of course language cannot be completely polarized in this way; it communicates across all kinds of difference, particularly that of gender. After all, men and women have always talked together, learned from each other, read each other's books. Any writer's style is the product of many different influences—temperament, situation and culture—which can never be disentangled. Yes, perhaps Sand wrote as she did partly because she was a woman, but she was also steeped in a male tradition, in the language of the male authors she read and loved—Montaigne, Rousseau, Chateaubriand, Hugo—and her style is equally formed by the structures and cadences of their sentences which remained in her mind. Many readers have seen her as transcending her sex, as a great writer not as a woman. Henry James (on certain occasions) was one of them, Flaubert another. Dostoyevsky called her 'une femme presque unique par la vigueur de son esprit et de son talent, un nom devenu désormais historique';[28] Matthew Arnold described her style as *'the large utterance of the early gods'*,[29] and Thackeray wrote of the charm of her 'brief rich melancholy sentences [...] they seem to me like the sound of country bells—provoking I don't know what vein of musing and meditation, and falling sweetly and sadly on the ear'.[30] Perhaps, then, she does achieve a kind of androgyny, sharing in a woman's world and a woman's language but not confined by them, attaining also an authority and elevation more usually described as male.

These judgements on Sand have for the most part been general observations; it is also necessary to look at the particular style and perspective of the *Histoire de ma vie*, since the voice she uses varies according to when a work was written and what its intended effect was. It is rare for Sand to allow any of her works to speak for itself. The narrator is clearly present in her novels too, addressing the reader directly, persuading him into agreement. Different perspectives are taken in different works; the story may be told from within, using one voice (as in *Mauprat* and *Les Maîtres sonneurs*) or many (as in *Lélia* or *Jacques*); most often the voice remains outside but is still evident and involved. When the speaker is a character in the plot, he is clearly a fictional construct, but as omniscient narrator, he is also far from being identical to the author. He is almost always male, superior to his characters, while often speaking for them, confident and worldly-wise. The narrator of Sand's autobiography coincides more nearly with the real person and is even more obvious, as the young protagonist· is seen almost exclusively through her eyes, the description of past experiences often acting as a trigger for deliberation on general issues. All autobiographies consist of alternating passages of narrative and reflection, but in the *Histoire* the emphasis is more clearly on present reflection. Indeed for Diane Johnson, it is paramount: 'Formal continuity is provided not by events but by a spiritual or mental theme, in the service of which "facts" can be bent a little.'[31] Sand has a similar view of the text's balance although she suggests no distortion: 'mon histoire par elle-même est fort peu intéressante. Les faits y jouent le moindre rôle, les réflexions la remplissent' (I, 27).

The weight accorded to the adult voice sets the tone of the text, gives it its immediacy, makes the reader feel involved in the very process of composition. Sand gives the impression of writing as she thinks; she is doubtful of certain dates, or has forgotten them (why didn't she look them up?), has just remembered a name which a few minutes earlier had eluded her: 'Madame Fontanier (voici que le nom de notre compagne de voyage me revient)' (I, 559). At one point on the same journey to Madrid, she wonders aloud where they were: 'Mais quel était cet endroit? Dieu le sait!' (I, 557). Elsewhere the flow of memory brings back an incident which happened much later in her story but which she relates now all the same, either because of its intrinsic interest or to bring the reader up to date: 'J'ai eu les derniers détails sur cet intérieur [of the convent] en 1847' (I, 1010). She may remember something but refuse to say what it is, tantalizing us with a foretaste of what is to come. When describing a scene from her mother's youth, for example, she says: 'le fait est certain, parce que Victoire ma mère me l'a dit, et dans des circonstances que je n'oublierai jamais: je raconterai cela en son lieu, mais je dois prier le lecteur de ne rien préjuger avant ma conclusion' (I, 73). In fact we are never told what these dramatic circumstances were but are left to read on in expectation to the end.

Sand as narrator, then, talks directly to us. Indeed this preference for an oral tone is often seen as a distinguishing feature of women's texts, since it is more immediate and personal—in keeping with our earlier account of female difference. An autobiographer of course needs to appeal to his readers directly since he depends more than a novelist on their acceptance of the autobiographical pact, their willingness to believe in what they are reading: 'the "I" is confirmed in the function of permanent subject by the presence of its correlative "you", giving clear motivation to the discourse.'[32] Only thus is the narrative authenticated, the aim of the autobiography, as witness, apology or self-defence, realized. The nature of the implied reader and of the narrator's relation to him/her will vary however from text to text. Some (male) autobiographers (Stendhal, Sartre), while pretending intimacy, keep an ironic distance, tease and unsettle, make us ponder on the moral message, even doubt the authenticity of what we are reading. Sand's address appears more intimate, more direct, to be taken literally, one might say, rather than figuratively.[33]

She begins by constructing her reader as a kind of mirror image of herself, 'Je sais bien que je n'écris pas pour le genre humain [...]. Les gens de mon métier n'écrivent jamais que pour un certain nombre de personnes placées dans des situations ou perdues dans des rêveries analogues à celles qui les occupent' (I, 21–2). Gender is irrelevant (although he is consistently referred to in the masculine). Despising the world and its doings, he is contemplative and idealistic, trusting feeling above all else; having suffered himself, he has an understanding of other people's suffering and will recognize his own story as he reads hers: 'Ecoutez; ma vie, c'est la vôtre' (I, 27). In this way, Sand makes us share her values, ensures we are reading in an appropriate frame of mind, preempts any disagreement. She then universalizes these same values in her description of her early years, setting them up as fundamental. We have all had idyllic childhoods: 'Il n'est pas un de nous qui ne se rappelle cet âge d'or comme un rêve évanoui' (I, 529), idyllic because then we lived more authentically, entirely through sensation and the imagination rather than through reason and common sense which she sees as blocking us off from the world. The reader is assumed to recognize himself again when she describes her adolescent experiments in writing as being typical of her generation. Here her address remains all-inclusive but is more closely linked to her time: 'j'ai lieu de croire que mon histoire intellectuelle est celle de la génération à laquelle j'appartiens, et qu'il n'est aucun de nous qui n'ait fait, dès son jeune âge, un roman ou un poème' (I, 808); she is not writing for posterity, aware perhaps that posterity is more difficult to convince. From this point on, her tone becomes increasingly defensive. As the behaviour she describes began to defy convention, she needs to appeal for understanding, rather than assuming it as her right. Her values and those of her implied reader are under attack by the world, are no longer obvious and universal. She returns to her stance at the beginning of the work—that she is writing only for like-minded souls—but now she is more outspoken; her reader has become her accomplice: 'Je n'écris pas pour me défendre de ceux qui ont un parti pris contre moi. J'écris pour ceux dont la sympathie naturelle, fondée sur une conformité d'instincts, m'ouvre le cœur et m'assure la confiance' (II, 94–5). Some pages later, she launches into an impassioned polemic on behalf of the oppressed and misunder-stood in order to work on the reader who by now has had his imagination stirred and conscience awakened. She uses the 'tu' form; her 'ami lecteur' has become her intimate, part of her, sharing her convictions, moved by her call to action. Although the passion soon subsides and the rhetoric disappears as the narrator returns to a more mundane account of her journey to Italy, the reader must remain persuaded in order to identify with and learn from her sufferings and desires to the end. Indeed she later assumes defiantly that all those she has failed to convince have stopped reading long ago: 'mon insistance sur les idées religieuses ennuiera donc beaucoup de personnes; mais je crois les avoir déjà assez ennuyées, depuis le commencement de cet ouvrage, pour qu'elles en aient, depuis longtemps, abandonné la lecture' (II, 306). Thus it is not only by deliberately tailoring her self-presentation to fit in with conventional expectations (as we saw in Chapter 1) that Sand ensures the appeal of her autobiography; it is also by the insidious use of a persuasive rhetoric which compels the reader into an appropriately responsive position.

It may be, however, that we are more effectively manipulated when Sand addresses us less explicitly. Our sympathies are perhaps better aroused by the direct and vivid evocation of experiences which affected her so deeply that she relived them as she wrote, from the heart not the head. The most important of these are associated with her mother (as described in Chapter 2), but there are other sensations and emotions from her childhood which are narrated with an unusual immediacy and sense of empathy with the little girl she was. We are drawn into her terror as the family crossed the dark forest near Orléans on the way to Paris, where she had seen a woman hanging from a tree, pecked at by crows, with her long black hair floating in the wind; and we identify with her hallucination when she dreamed she was the guardian angel of Napoleon's army, flying above it as it retreated through the bare, white Russian steppes. Certain scenes from her adolescence are equally memorable for her and for the reader, such as the last evening before her grandmother suffered the stroke from which she never fully recovered: 'Je me souviens que cette nuit-là fut extraordinairement belle et douce. Il faisait un clair de lune voilé par ces petits nuages blancs que Chateaubriand comparait à des flocons de ouate. Je ne travaillai point, je laissai ma fenêtre ouverte et jouai de la harpe' (I, 1030). There is no sentimentality in these passages, no self-consciousness; their intensity lies in their clarity and simplicity unembellished by hindsight. Sand has the gift of recreating what it feels like to be a child, particularly a little girl or young woman, whose sensibility is easily stimulated and whose nerves are often on edge. The vividness of such descriptions is intensified by being contrasted with the mediocre ugliness of the present day as, in Proustian fashion, the adult narrator revisits the haunts of her childhood and feels only sadness and loss. Her grandmother's apartment in Paris is now 'noir, sale, enfumé et puant le caporal, au lieu des exquises senteurs de ma grand-mère [...]. Mon cœur se serra de retrouver si laide, si triste et si sombre cette habitation toute pleine de mes souvenirs' (I, 727).

It is possible to link to Sand's gender such stylistic features as we have just described—the immediacy and orality of her discourse, her conversational intimacy with the reader, even her need to manipulate him from her position of oppression, and her ease of access into the world of childhood—although they are obviously also present in some works by some men. In other ways, however, the language of the *Histoire* goes far beyond such gender stereotyping to embrace styles and perspectives found in all kinds of texts. Although the narrator's tendency to digress may remind us of a 'feminine' unmediated discourse which follows a train of thought, the tone and content of the digressions situate Sand clearly outside a woman's conventional position. By constantly straying from the point, she does give us the sense of a mind which is alive and free, an impression which is reinforced by the way topics can straddle chapter divisions so that the narrating voice is continuous like life. Yet most often these reflective passages imply on Sand's part an assumption of wisdom more usually thought of as 'male'. The digression may have as its starting point an experience shared with the reader—her relations with her servants, the kindness of her Jesuit confessor—but it then moves into a broader perspective which brings the past into the present and extends the individual to the universal, as the language becomes more authoritative and abstract. Thus Sand moralizes at length on a variety of subjects, peasant superstition, education, the right to property, the nature of friendship, at risk sometimes of drowning the narrative of her past life in a welter of abstract generalities. Although fully aware of this danger, she saw such a style as integral to her purpose, as an essential part of her self-presentation: 'je me suis permis une fois pour toutes les interminables digressions' (I, 18), for which she only pretends to apologize: 'Voilà une bien longue digression, mais je la crois utile pour tout le monde' (I, 773).

At other times, particularly in the first two-thirds of her story up to her departure for Paris, Sand takes up the opposite stance, that of the (male) realist novelist rather than the thinker and moralizer, equally authoritative and omniscient but concerned with the concrete not the abstract. She uses many well-tried fictional techniques, perhaps most obviously when she retells incidents that she had heard from others, her mother or her tutor, transforming them with her novelist's art into striking, dramatic tales and giving us narrative at a second remove. For example, when describing how Deschartres and the young Maurice (her father) stole back some vital papers during Madame Dupin's imprisonment by the Revolutionary powers, she plays up the suspense by accumulating the verbs in the historic present, and giving the characters' thoughts in free indirect style: 'Alors tous deux, dans le plus complet silence, se mettent à l'œuvre. L'examen des papiers continue et marche rapidement; on brûle à mesure; mais quoi! quatre heures sonnent! Il faudra plus d'une heure pour refermer les portes et replacer les scellés. La moitié de la besogne n'est pas faite, et à cinq heures le citoyen Leblanc est invariablement debout' (I, 67). Later on, she thinks herself into the minds of her parents, recreating a poignant and macabre conversation on the evening after the death of their baby son, which led to his being exhumed and reburied. She dramatizes the climaxes of her own life in the same way as an alternative to introspective analysis which might become monotonous. She puts words into her young mouth, in order to play up a confrontation, give herself a heroine's stature (as well as to move the reader more directly), thus giving the 'truth' the aura of fiction. In defence of Deschartres, for example, accused of embezzlement, or in an appeal to Madame Alicia to treat her as an adopted daughter, she speaks with an eloquence and self-confidence beyond her years: 'Je ne sais pas encore ce que je suis et ce que je peux être. Je sens que je vous aime beaucoup, et je me figure que, de quelque façon que je tourne, vous serez forcée de m'aimer aussi' (I, 923).

She is not always so melodramatic; she can also act as objective chronicler of her times. She brings out the horror of the cholera which struck Paris in May 1832 and of the insurrection the following month, not by exaggerating it but through a vivid, factual description of the funeral processions which passed outside the window of her attic flat on the quai St Michel:

ce qu'il y avait de plus effrayant, ce n'était pas ces morts entassés pêle-mêle comme des ballots, c'était l'absence des parents et des amis derrière les chars funèbres; c'était les conducteurs doublant le pas, jurant et fouettant les chevaux; c'était les passants s'éloignant avec effroi du hideux cortège; c'était la rage des ouvriers qui croyaient à une fantastique mesure d'empoisonnement et qui levaient leurs poings fermés contre le ciel; c'était, quand ces groupes menaçants avaient passé, l'abattement ou l'insouciance qui rendaient toutes les physionomies irritantes ou stupides. (II, 142)

The atmosphere of suffering mingled with indifference is implied through the accumulation of expressive detail and through the rhythm of the sentence whose rise and fall mimics the sound of the hearses as they rumble past and then fade away.

The passages describing Sand's childhood pranks in Nohant with her half-brother, Hippolyte, the practical jokes he played on Deschartres, are equally realistic and convincing, although in a comic not a serious vein. For Sand also brings out the funny side of things: of an extraordinary contraption invented by her writing teacher to force her into the right posture, of Casimir's matter-of-fact approach when courting her, of a night walk with Balzac wearing his dressing-gown. She may use a playful, self-deprecating tone when describing the dreams of her younger self as 'le plus étrange gâchis poétique' (I, 541), for example; and her portraits of the 'vieilles comtesses', friends of her grandmother, brilliantly capture their bizarre, outdated appearance and eccentric mannerisms, and are as successful in their way as some of Balzac's more hyperbolic creations. It is possible that Proust was inspired by them in his evocation of a similarly decadent and anachronistic society.[34]

Sand's style and perspective, then, vary constantly. The *Histoire de ma vie* appears as an amalgam of different voices, detached and spontaneous, public and private, male and female. Personal confession, philosophical meditation, historical document, realistic memoir, it has something of all of these and in this way corresponds more directly to the multiple, ambiguous and androgynous identity of its author, as she was and as she wished to appear.

Notes to Chapter 4

1. Sheringham, *French Autobiography*, 21.
2. Henry James, *French Writers, Other European Writers, Prefaces to the New York edition* (New York: The Library of America, 1986), 702.
3. Ruth Jordan, *George Sand: a biography* (London: Constable, 1976), p. xv.
4. See Ch. 1, pt. 2, for a fuller discussion of how she presents her younger self.
5. Anne Freadman, 'Of cats and companions and the name of George Sand', in *Grafts: Feminist Cultural Criticism*, ed. Susan Sheridan (London: Verso, 1988), 137.
6. Sand, *Correspondance*, iii. 490.
7. Nicole Mozet, 'Signé "le voyageur": George Sand et l'invention de l'artiste', *Romantisme* 55 (1987), 27.
8. Avron Fleishman, *Figures of Autobiography: the Language of Self-writing* (Berkeley: University of California Press, 1983), 35.
9. Woolf, *A Room of One's Own*, 100

10. Woolf, *A Room of One's Own*, 112.
11. Hélène Cixous, 'Le Rire de la Méduse', *L'Arc* 61 (1975), 43.
12. See Luce Irigaray, *Ce Sexe qui n'en est pas un* (Paris: Editions de Minuit, 1977).
13. Julia Kristeva, *La Révolution du langage poétique* (Paris: Seuil, 1974), 26.
14. Margaret Homans, *Bearing the Word: Language and Female Experience in Nineteenth-Century Women's Writing* (Chicago: University of Chicago Press, 1986), 14.
15. The link is made by Pierrette Daly in 'De Sand à Cixous', *Colloque de Cérisy*, ed. Simone Vierne (Paris: Sedes, 1983).
16. Sand, *Correspondance*, xx. 217.
17. See *George Sand Papers: Conference Proceedings* (New York: AMS Press Inc., 1976), 96.
18. Quoted by André Fermigier in his Preface to *François le Champi* (Paris: Gallimard, 1976), 9.
19. Baudelaire, *Œuvres complètes*, i. 686.
20. Baudelaire, *Œuvres complètes*, ii. 282–3.
21. James, *French Writers, Other European Writers*, 760.
22. James, *French Writers, Other European Writers*, 721.
23. Baudelaire, *Œuvres complètes*, ii. 145.
24. See Françoise van Rossum-Guyon, 'A propos d'Indiana', *Colloque de Cérisy*, ed. Vierne (Paris: Sedes, 1983), 76.
25. See Anne Berger, 'Let's go to the fountain; on George Sand and writing', in *Writing Differences: Readings from the seminar of Hélène Cixous*, ed. Susan Sellers (New York: St Martin's Press, 1988).
26. Sand, *Correspondance*, ii. 135–6.
27. Several critics, however, point out the many masculine images which Sand also uses to describe her writing practice, and the numerous references in her letters to the killing burden that the necessity to write placed upon her. See Naginski, *George Sand, Writing for her Life*, 221–6 ; Donna Dickenson, *George Sand: a Brave Man, the Most Womanly Woman*, and Francine Mallet, *George Sand* (Paris: Grasset, 1995).
28. Quoted by Wladimir Karénine, *George Sand, sa vie et ses œuvres* (Paris: Paul Ollendorf, 1899), i. 34.
29. Quoted by Patricia Thomson, *George Sand and the Victorians* (Plymouth: Bowering Press, 1977), 94.
30. Thomson, *George Sand and the Victorians*, 19.
31. Diane Johnson, 'Experience as melodrama', in *Terrorists and Novelists* (New York: Alfred A. Knopf, 1982), 44.
32. Jean Starobinski, 'The Style of Autobiography', in *Autobiography; Essays Theoretical and Critical*, ed. Olney, 77.
33. See reference earlier in this chapter to Homans, *Bearing the Word*.
34. Pierre-Edmond Robert, 'George Sand's Presence in Proust's *A la Recherche du temps perdu*', in *West Virginia George Sand Conference Papers*, ed. Armand Singer (Morgantown, West Virginia: Dept. of Foreign Languages, West Virginia University, 1981), 57–8.

CONCLUSION

Having examined the *Histoire de ma vie* from many different points of view, having discussed the various identities it projects (small child, adolescent girl, young woman, mature writer), the shape the narrative adopts and the tone of its writing, I would hope we have come closer to understanding the person of its author, not least through the ways in which she attempts to accommodate her own particularity within accepted models of autobiographical writing. The resulting text has a certain hybrid quality, which is itself revealing, although it still leaves Sand's contradictions, particularly those of gender, largely unresolved. If, however, we take a final look at the *Histoire*, we may be struck by the recurrence of certain privileged images which because of the special intensity of their expression allow us a unique, imaginative access to the child and woman that she 'really' was. They are all images of place, 'images de l'*espace heureux*', as Bachelard calls them,[1] which correspond to Sand's most basic aspirations as she both experienced and remembers them, and in particular to her finding of herself. The estate of Nohant is of course fundamental at her beginning and her end, as she explains early on in the *Histoire*: 'Je dirai quelques mots de cette terre de Nohant où j'ai été élevée, où j'ai passé presque toute ma vie et où je souhaiterais pouvoir mourir' (I, 122). Paris, its opposite, was equally central and indispensable to her self-construction since here she found the space to grow beyond the family circle. Her autobiography traces that coming and going between these two essential points which began in her childhood and lasted all her life. Yet within this alternation and set apart from it, there are two other, smaller, favoured spaces which Sand presents as directly symbolic of her inner world and expressive of her two opposing but essential needs: the garden and the room of her own. Passionate, lyrical descriptions of both these reappear throughout the *Histoire*, as places where she felt happiest and most at peace. Taken together, they encapsulate the essential duality in her personality which we have seen earlier in different features of the text—that is, her two contrasting attitudes to her womanhood: an instinctive closeness to nature and a need to go beyond her sex.

Many autobiographies, and novels too, exploit the archetypal image of the garden as an enclosed, paradisal space which the protagonist must leave in order to discover himself and the world. This is its meaning for Sand too, but she gives it a peculiarly feminine twist, not just because Nature is conventionally associated with woman, but because for her the garden clearly represents more specifically the ideal of a harmonious and happy family life, often centred on the figure of the mother, for which she yearned all her life. In the garden, woman is in her rightful place, as mother, daughter, sister, not temptress and seducer. (Sand's view of the garden is not orthodoxly Christian, for she had little sense of original sin and seems not to have believed in the Fall.) The first garden to appear in the *Histoire* belonged to her aunt at Chaillot whom the child visited with her mother during those very early years in the Paris flat. It is the original Eden—'à peine avais-je mis le pied dans le jardin, que je me croyais dans l'île enchantée de mes contes' (I, 544)—where she played with her sister and her cousin, chasing after butterflies and wondering at the threads of gossamer shimmering in the autumn sunshine. The much larger garden at Nohant, with its lawns, huge, overarching trees and winding paths repeats and amplifies the same theme, for it combines the figure of the mother (as we saw in Chapter 2) with the sisterly presence of Ursule, the little village girl who was brought in to keep Aurore company and shared in the mother's construction of the enchanted grotto, whose magic neither her half-brother nor her grandmother understood.

The young girl was equally happy in the garden of the convent, within a larger community of mothers and sisters, although here the garden is only one part of the secluded Paradise that the whole convent represented for her. It is, however, the park at Le Plessis, where she stayed after her grandmother's death, which appears most clearly as the Garden of Eden of her dreams. Like the convent, but described at much greater length, it is set apart from her normal life and has none of the unhappy associations of Nohant; it is a green and fertile place, full of fruit, flowers and trees, resounding with the laughter of children and young people, and watched over by the benevolent Du Plessis couple:

Je croyais n'aimer que Nohant. Le Plessis s'empara de moi comme un Eden [...]. Tout cela était moins rustique, mieux tenu, mieux distribué, partant moins pittoresque et moins rêveur que Nohant; mais quelles longues voûtes de branches, quelles perspectives de verdure, quels beaux temps de galop dans les allées sablonneuses! Et puis des hôtes jeunes, des figures toujours gaies, des enfants terribles si bons enfants! [...] C'était la véritable partie de plaisir, l'amusement à plusieurs, la vie de famille pour laquelle, sans m'en douter, j'étais si bien faite. (II, 17–18)

As a young wife and mother herself, she returned to Le Plessis a few years later in the hope of recapturing her earlier happiness, but her husband is now critical of her childish games—'mon mari [...] me jugea idiote' (II, 42)—and the idyll is rudely cut short. She attempted a pale imitation of it in one final garden, at d'Ormesson just outside Paris, whither the couple had fled from the tête-à-tête at Nohant which they now dreaded, and where she spent hours reading and playing with her young son; but this fragile paradise of mother and child was also destroyed by a male voice, that of the gardener who roughly admonished her for damage done to the plants so that she was frightened to go back.

The image of the garden does not appear in the later part of the text as Sand's dream of a conventional womanly happiness failed (although in her old age, after the *Histoire* was written, she may have recaptured it with her grandchildren at Nohant). It is replaced by its opposite, the separate and solitary place which drove her back on herself. Since Virginia Woolf, a preoccupation with 'a room of one's own' has also been seen as primarily and necessarily feminine, as a woman's act of defiance against a male world which denies her her own private place, assuming she has no needs beyond those of her family. Although a room apart could be construed as a prison and a place of exile (as Elaine Showalter suggests),[2] there is no doubt that Sand's first experience of it, when she was given her own cell at the convent, was uniquely joyous. Tiny and uncomfortable as it was, directly beneath the roof, like an oven in summer and an icebox in winter, she loved it with passion. She was in the world but not of it, dominating it from her window which overlooked the convent buildings and the roofs of Paris, listening to its distant murmur as she lay in bed, with only the birds as visitors and companions.[3] She savoured her isolation, away from the constant company of her convent sisters which she found confining as well as delightful. Here she could be and do exactly as she wanted: 'Je ne saurais dire quel monde de rêveries semblait lié pour moi à cette petite niche poudreuse et misérable. C'est là seulement que je me retrouvais et que je m'appartenais' (I, 945).

The same pressing need for solitude reappears ten years or so later, when she was once more living a communal life, now with her husband and children at Nohant; again she found a place apart, but within hearing distance of her children whose bedroom was next to hers. She took over the tiny room which had been her grandmother's boudoir, thus carving out a rather uneasy space for herself within her family but separate from it. She filled it so full of her furniture and possessions that she was obliged, as she puts it, to write in a cupboard (II, 100). It was here that she composed *Indiana* and *Valentine*, thus making the link between seclusion, self-possession and literary creation which is at the origin of Woolf's privileging of the 'room of one's own'.

Later in the *Histoire* there appears a whole series of 'maisons désertes' as they have now become, empty houses which Sand sought out wherever she happened to be, particularly during the troubled period of her legal proceedings against her husband. Here she found a refuge not just from her immediate family but from a whole society in which she had become a well-known figure. She was no longer able to integrate her private space into her everyday life as she had at the convent and at Nohant, and now could withdraw only briefly, although more completely, for a vital period of contemplation and renewal. The most extended description of such a place in the *Histoire* appears in connection with her temporary occupation of a flat in Paris which was in the process of being renovated. Nobody knew she was there; she shared her living space only with the spiders, the mice and the birds. As at the convent, the muted sounds from the street reinforced her delight in her own solitude. The flat was in a kind of limbo, between occupancies, and her life too had stopped, giving her the space to write: 'Le moindre coin nous devient alors une prison volontaire, et, quel qu'il soit, il se pare à nos yeux de ce je ne sais quoi de délicieux qui est comme le sentiment de la conquête et de la possession du temps, du silence et de nous-mêmes' (II, 347). She discovered the same happiness and peace in an empty house at Bourges later in the same year, rapidly mentioned in the *Histoire*, and described at length in the seventh *Lettre d'un voyageur*, where the 'maison déserte' is most clearly presented as fulfilling a fundamental emotional need.

The image takes a slightly different form when the 'maison déserte' is Nohant itself, which Sand briefly occupied alone during the separation proceedings. Once again, she revelled in the sense of space as well as the solitude; for none of these 'maisons désertes' contained the clutter of the convent cell or the 'cupboard' where she used to write, as though the adult needed more room to breathe physically in order to be able to breathe spiritually. But Nohant was not anonymous; on the contrary it was full of personal memories, which she deliberately awakened by replacing the furniture as it had been in her youth, and walking through the darkened house, allowing her spirit to withdraw into itself in order to be able to expand into the past and reintegrate her younger being:

J'allumais beaucoup de bougies et je me promenais dans l'enfilade de grandes pièces du rez-de-chaussée, depuis le petit boudoir où je couchais toujours, jusqu'au grand salon illuminé en outre par un grand feu. Puis j'éteignais tout, et marchant à la seule lueur du feu mourant de l'âtre, je savourais l'émotion de cette obscurité mystérieuse et pleine de pensées mélancoliques, après avoir ressaisi les riants et doux souvenirs de mes jeunes années. (II, 377)¹

It is easy to see the images of the garden and the room/'maison déserte' as opposite sides of the same coin: outside and inside, expansion and withdrawal, multitude and solitude, the physical and the mental, loss of self and reintegration of self. There is one place which appears in Sand's autobiography as combining the characteristics of both and so as peculiarly blessed. It has something in common with the pavilion in *Valentine* which Nancy Miller also sees as symbolic, integrating the private with the public, the emotional with the artistic, a place where classes and genders can mix equally and where nobody is confined within a stereotype.⁴ But this is a fictional ideal; its parallel in the *Histoire* remains a personal, solitary dream of the young Aurore, recollected with nostalgia and a certain humorous disenchantment by the adult narrator. For in the temple the child raised to Corambé in the park at Nohant, all the richly privileged imagery associated with gardens is brought together: at its origin is the grotto built for her by her mother, of whom Corambé is partly an incarnation. It is similarly formed from the green branches of trees, carpeted with moss, decorated with shells and garlands of flowers. Then, it is also a secluded enclosure, a place apart, difficult of access, in the heart of a near-impenetrable thicket, into which the child could withdraw to escape from the real world and dream:

'Quand tout fut prêt, je pris possession de mon empire avec délices, et, m'asseyant sur la mousse, je me mis à rêver' (I, 820). This synthesis, this perfect place has also a divine dimension, which elevates it above the other more worldly spaces: it is a temple with an altar to which angels might descend and at which religious rites are performed. But like the grotto and the garden at Le Plessis, like the pavilion, its magic also is destroyed by an alien (male) presence; once it had been discovered by Liset, the little peasant boy who was Aurore's companion, she wanted only to dismantle it, ceremonially burying the garlands and shells beneath the ruins of the altar.

Although a childish fantasy of the little girl, the garden temple fulfilled two essential needs which Sand felt all her life; hence its clear links with other places and other aspects of her self-presentation, and the vivid detail in which it is described. Of course, the garden and the solitary retreat are archetypal images of different forms of perfect, often divine, happiness which appear in literary texts of all kinds. Their centrality in Sand's *Histoire* ties her into a cultural, Judeo-Christian tradition which is broadly human; but since this is an autobiographical text, the images which it privileges correspond also to the actual experience of its author, and it is this which at least in part gives them their distinctive form. Sand makes them uniquely expressive of what we have identified as her fundamental dilemma: how to enjoy the womanly happiness of communion with a family while at the same time fulfilling her private need for solitude and mental expansion, how to be both a woman and more than a woman.

Notes to Conclusion

1. Gaston Bachelard, *La Poétique de l'espace* (Paris: Presses Universitaires de France, 1958), 17.
2. Elaine Showalter, *A Literature of their Own: British Women Novelists from Brontë to Lessing* (Princeton: Princeton University Press, 1977), 285.
3. See Jeanne Goldin, 'Du couvent à la chambre à soi', in *George Sand Today*, ed. David A. Powell (Lanham, New York and London: University Press of America, 1992), 68.
4. Nancy K. Miller, 'Writing (from) the Feminine: George Sand and the novel of female pastoral', in *The Representation of Women in Fiction*, ed. Carolyn G. Heilbrun and Margaret R. Higonnet (Baltimore: Johns Hopkins University Press, 1983), 124–51.

BIBLIOGRAPHY

Works by George Sand

Consuelo, La Comtesse de Rudolfstadt (1842, 1844; Paris: Garnier, 1959).
Correspondance, ed. Georges Lubin, 25 vols. (Paris: Garnier, 1964–90).
François le Champi (1847; Paris: Gallimard, 1975).
Indiana (1832; Paris: Gallimard, 1984).
Lélia (1833; Paris: Garnier, 1960).
Mauprat (1837; Paris: Gallimard, 1981).
Œuvres autobiographiques, ed. Georges Lubin, 2 vols. (Paris: Gallimard, Bibliothèque de la Pléiade, 1970–1).
La Petite Fadette (1848; Paris: Garnier, 1981).
Valentine (1832; Paris: Editions de l'Aurore, 1988).

Books and articles on George Sand

ASTMAN, JOSEPH G. (ed.), *George Sand Conference Proceedings, 1976, 78, 80, 82, 86* (New York: AMS Press).
BARRY, JOSEPH, *Infamous Woman: the Life of George Sand* (New York: Doubleday, 1977).
BERGER, ANNE, 'Let's go to the fountain; on George Sand and writing', in *Writing Differences: Readings from the Seminar of Hélène Cixous*, ed. Susan Sellers (New York: St Martin's Press, 1988), 54–65.
BOSSIS, MIREILLE, 'Les Relations de parenté chez George Sand', *Cahiers de l'Association Internationale des Etudes françaises* 28 (May 1976), 297–314.
BOUCHARDEAU, HUGUETTE, *George Sand, la lune et les sabots* (Paris: Robert Laffont, 1990).
BOZON-SCALZETTI, YVETTE, 'Vérité de la fiction et fiction de la vérité dans *Histoire de ma vie*', *Nineteenth-Century French Studies* 13 (1984), 95–118.
BRÉE, GERMAINE, 'George Sand: The fictions of autobiography', *Nineteenth-Century French Studies* 4 (1976), 438–49.
—— 'Le Mythe des origines et l'autoportrait chez George Sand et Colette', in *Symposium and Modern Literature: Studies in Honour of Wallace Fowlie*, ed. Marcel Tetel (Durham, North Carolina: Duke University Press, 1978), 103–12.

CATE, CURTIS, *George Sand: a Biography* (New York: Avon, 1975).

CELLIER, L. (ed.), *Hommage à George Sand* (Paris: Presses Universitaires de France, 1969).

CRECELIUS, KATHRYN J., *Family Romances: George Sand's Early Novels* (Bloomington: Indiana University Press, 1987).

DATLOF, NATHALIE, FUCHS, JEANNE, and POWELL, DAVID A. (eds.), *The World of George Sand* (Westport: Greenwood Press, 1991).

DEUTELBAUM, WENDY, and HUFF, CYNTHIA, 'Class, gender and family system: the case of George Sand', in *The M/other Tongue: Essays in Feminist Psychoanalytic Interpretation*, ed. Shirley Nelson Garner, Claire Kahane and Madelon Sprengnether (Ithaca, New York: Cornell University Press, 1985), 260–79.

DEUTSCH, HELENE, *The Psychology of Women: A Psychoanalytic Interpretation*, vol. i (London: Research Books, 1946).

DICKENSON, DONNA, *George Sand: a Brave Man, the Most Womanly Woman* (Oxford: Berg, 1988).

DIDIER, BÉATRICE, 'Femme en voyage', in *L'Ecriture femme* (Paris: Presses Universitaires de France, 1981), 131–207.

—— 'Femme/Identité/Ecriture: à propos de *L'Histoire de ma vie* de George Sand', *Revue des Sciences humaines* (Oct.–Dec. 1977), 561–76.

—— and NEEFS, JACQUES (eds.), *George Sand: Ecritures du romantisme* ii (Saint Denis: Presses Universitaires de Vincennes, 1989).

—— *George Sand écrivain "Un grand fleuve d'Amérique"* (Paris: Presses Universitaires de France, 1998).

FRAPPIER-MAZUR, LUCIENNE, 'Nostalgie, dédoublement et écriture dans *Histoire de ma vie*', *Nineteenth-Century French Studies* 17 (1989), 265–74.

FREADMAN, ANNE, 'Of cats and companions and the name of George Sand', in *Grafts: Feminist Cultural Criticism*, ed. Susan Sheridan (London: Verso, 1988), 125–56.

GLASGOW, JANIS (ed.), *George Sand: Collected Essays* (New York: Whitston Publishing Company, 1985).

JAMES, HENRY, *French Poets and Novelists* (London: Macmillan, 1884), 149–85.

—— *French Writers, Other European Writers, Prefaces to the New York Edition* (New York: The Library of America, 1984), 696–798.

JOHNSON, DIANE, 'Experience as melodrama: George Sand', in *Terrorists and Novelists* (New York: Alfred A. Knopf, 1982), 41–51.

JORDAN, RUTH, *George Sand: a Biographical Portrait* (London: Constable, 1976).

JURGRAU, THELMA, 'Autobiography in general and George Sand in particular', *Nineteenth-Century French Studies* 17 (1988), 196–207.

—— (ed.), *Story of my Life*, a group translation (Albany: State University of New York Press, 1990).

KARÉNINE, WLADIMIR, *George Sand, sa vie et ses œuvres,* 4 vols. (Paris: Paul Ollendorf, 1899).

L'HÔPITAL, MADELEINE, *La Notion de l'artiste chez George Sand* (Paris: Boivin, 1956).

MACLEAN, MARIE, *The Name of the Mother: Writing Illegitimacy* (London: Routledge, 1994), 64–86.

MALLET, FRANCINE, *George Sand* (Paris: Grasset, 1976, rev. edn 1995).

MILLER, NANCY K., 'Women's autobiography in France: for a Dialectics of Identification', in *Women and Language in Literature and Society,* ed. Sally McConnell Ginet, Ruth Borker and Nelly Furman (Westport: Praeger Publishers, 1980), 258–73.

—— 'Writing (from) the Feminine: George Sand and the novel of female pastoral,' in *The Representation of Women in Fiction,* ed. Carolyn G. Heilbrun and Margaret R. Higonnet (Baltimore: Johns Hopkins University Press, 1983), 124–51.

—— *Subject to Change: Reading Feminist writing* (New York: Columbia University Press, 1988), 77–101.

MOERS, ELLEN, *Literary Women: The Great Writers* (New Jersey: Doubleday, Anchor Books, 1977).

MOZET, NICOLE, 'Signé "le voyageur": George Sand et l'invention de l'artiste', *Romantisme* 55 (1987), 23–32.

NAGINSKI, ISABELLE HOOG, *George Sand: Writing for her Life* (New Brunswick: Rutgers University Press, 1991).

POWELL, DAVID A., *George Sand* (Boston: Twayne Publishers, 1990).

—— (ed.), *George Sand Today: Proceedings of International George Sand Conference* (Lanham, New York and London: University Press of America, 1989, 1992).

RABINE, LESLEY, 'Feminist writers in French Romanticism', *Studies in Romanticism* 16 (1977), 491–507.

ROGERS, NANCY, 'Psychosexual identity and the erotic imagination in the early novels of George Sand', *Studies in Literary Imagination* 12 (1979), 19–35.

SCHAEFFER, GERALD, *Espace et temps chez George Sand* (Neuchâtel: La Baconnière, 1981).

SCHOR, NAOMI, 'Reading double: George Sand and difference,' in *The Poetics of Gender,* ed. Nancy K. Miller (New York: Columbia University Press, 1986), 248–69.

—— *George Sand and Idealism* (New York: Columbia University Press, 1993).

SINGER, ARMAND E., *West Virginia George Sand Conference Papers* (Morgantown, West Virginia: Department of Foreign Languages, West Virginia University, 1981).

THOMSON, PATRICIA, *George Sand and the Victorians: Her Influence and*

Reputation in Nineteenth-Century England (London: Macmillan, 1977).

VAN ROSSUM-GUYON, FRANÇOISE (ed.), *George Sand: recherches nouvelles* (Amsterdam, 1983).

—— *Une œuvre multiforme: recherches nouvelles* ii (Amsterdam, 1991, 1995).

VIERNE, SIMONE (ed.), *Colloque de Cérisy* (Paris: Sedes, 1983).

General books and articles

ABEL, ELIZABETH, HIRSCH, MARIANNE, and LANGLAND, ELIZABETH (eds.), *The Voyage In: Fictions of Female Development* (Hanover and London: published for Dartmouth College, University Press of New England, 1983).

ALBISTUR, MAITÉ, and ARMOGATHE, DANIEL, *Histoire du féminisme français du moyen âge à nos jours* (Paris: Edition des Femmes, 1977).

BACHELARD, GASTON, *La Poétique de l'espace* (Paris: Presses Universitaires de France, 1958).

BAUDELAIRE, CHARLES, *Œuvres complètes*, 2 vols. (Paris: Gallimard, Bibliothèque de la Pléiade, 1976).

DE BEAUVOIR, SIMONE, *Le Deuxième Sexe* (Paris: Gallimard, 1949).

—— *Mémoires d'une jeune fille rangée* (Paris: Gallimard, 1958).

—— *La Force de l'âge* (Paris: Gallimard, 1960).

—— *La Force des choses* (Paris: Gallimard, 1963).

BENSTOCK, SHARI (ed.), *The Private Self: Theory and Practice of Women's Autobiographical Writings* (London: Routledge, 1988).

BLAU DU PLESSIS, RACHEL, *Writing beyond the Ending* (Bloomington: Indiana University Press, 1985).

CHATEAUBRIAND, FRANÇOIS-RENÉ DE, *Mémoires d'outre-tombe* (Paris: Gallimard, Bibliothèque de la Pléiade, 1951).

CHODOROW, NANCY, *The Reproduction of Mothering: Psychoanalysis and the Sociology of Gender* (Berkeley: University of California Press, 1978).

CIXOUS, HÉLÈNE, 'Le Rire de la Méduse', *L'Arc* 61 (1975).

COE, RICHARD, *When the Grass was Taller: Autobiography and the Experience of Childhood* (New Haven: Yale University Press, 1984).

DE JEAN, JOAN, and MILLER, NANCY K. (eds.), *Displacements: Women, Tradition, Literature in French* (Baltimore: Johns Hopkins University Press, 1991).

EAKIN, PAUL JOHN, *Fictions in Autobiography: Studies in the Art of Self-Invention* (Princeton: Princeton University Press, 1985).

FLEISHMAN, AVRON, *Figures of Autobiography: the Language of Self-Writing* (Berkeley: University of California Press, 1983).

FREUD, SIGMUND, 'Beyond the Pleasure Principle' and 'Femininity', in *The Essentials of Psychoanalysis* (Harmondsworth: Penguin Books, 1991), 218–68, 412–32.

GILBERT, SANDRA, and GUBAR, SUSAN, *The Madwoman in the Attic: the Woman Writer and the Nineteenth-Century Literary Imagination* (New Haven: Yale University Press, 1979).

—— 'Sexual Linguistics: gender, language and sexuality', *New Literary History* (Spring 1985).

GUNN, JANET VARNER, *Towards a Poetics of Experience* (Philadelphia: University of Pennsylvania Press, 1982).

HEILBRUN, CAROLYN G., *Towards Androgyny: Aspects of Male and Female in Literature* (London: Gollancz, 1973).

—— *Writing a Woman's Life* (London: Woman's Press, 1989).

HERRMAN, CLAUDINE, *Les Voleuses de langue* (Paris: Editions des Femmes, 1976).

HIRSCH, MARIANNE, *The Mother/Daughter Plot* (Bloomington: Indiana University Press, 1989).

HOMANS, MARGARET, *Women Writers and Poetic Identity* (Princeton: Princeton University Press, 1980).

—— *Bearing the Word; Language and Female Experience in Nineteenth-Century Women's Writing* (Chicago: University of Chicago Press, 1986).

IRIGARAY, LUCE, *Ce Sexe qui n'en est pas un* (Paris: Editions de Minuit, 1977).

JAY, PAUL L., 'Being in the text: autobiography and the problem of the subject', *Modern Language Notes* 97 (Dec. 1982), 1045–63.

JELINEK, ESTELLE C. (ed.), *Women's Autobiography: Essays in Criticism* (Bloomington: Indiana University Press, 1980).

—— *The Tradition of Women's Autobiography; from Antiquity to the Present* (Boston: Twayne Publishers, 1986).

KING, ADÈLE, *French Women Novelists: Defining a Female Style* (London: Macmillan, 1989).

KRISTEVA, JULIA, *La Révolution du langage poétique* (Paris: Seuil, 1974).

LACAN, JACQUES, *Le Séminaire livre XI, Les quatre concepts fondamentaux de l* psychanalyse (Paris: Seuil, 1973).

LEJEUNE, PHILIPPE, *L'Autobiographie en France* (Paris: Armand Colin, 1971).

—— *Le Pacte autobiographique* (Paris: Seuil, 1975).

DE MAN, PAUL, 'Autobiography as de-facement', *Modern Language Notes* 94 (1979), 99–130.

MAY, GEORGES, *L'Autobiographie en France* (Paris: Presses Universitaires de France, 1979).

MOI, TORIL, *Sexual/Textual Politics: Feminist Literary Theory* (London: Methuen, 1985).

OLNEY, JAMES, *Metaphors of Self; the Meaning of Autobiography* (Princeton: Princeton University Press, 1972).

—— (ed.), *Autobiography; Essays Theoretical and Critical* (Princeton: Princeton University Press, 1980).

—— (ed.), *Studies in Autobiography* (Oxford: Oxford University Press, 1988).

PASCAL, ROY, *Design and Truth in Autobiography* (London: Routledge and Kegan Paul, 1960).

PIKE, BURTON, 'Time in autobiography', *Comparative Literature* 28 (1976), 326–42.

PLANTÉ, CHRISTINE, *La Petite Sœur de Balzac; essai sur la femme auteur* (Paris: Seuil, 1989).

MADAME ROLAND, *Mémoires* (Paris: Mercure de France, 1960).

ROUSSEAU, JEAN-JACQUES, *Confessions* (Paris: Gallimard, Bibliothèque de la Pléiade, 1959).

SARTORI, E. M., and ZIMMERMAN, D. W. (eds.), *French Women Writers: a Bio-bibliographical Source Book* (Westport: Greenwood Press, 1991).

SARTRE, JEAN-PAUL, *Les Mots* (Paris: Gallimard, 1964).

SCHENCK, CELESTE M., and BRODZKI, BELLA (eds.), *Life/Lines; Theorizing Women's Autobiography* (Ithaca: Cornell University Press, 1988).

SELLERS, SUSAN, *Language and Sexual Difference; Feminist Writing in France* (London: Macmillan, 1991).

SHAPIRO, STEVEN, 'The Dark Continent of literary autobiography', *Comparative Literary Studies* 5 (1968), 421–54.

SHERINGHAM, MICHAEL, *French Autobiography: Devices and Desires* (Oxford: Clarendon Press, 1993).

SHOWALTER, ELAINE, *A Literature of their Own: British Women Novelists from Brontë to Lessing* (Princeton: Princeton University Press, 1977).

SMITH, SIDONIE, *A Poetics of Women's Autobiography* (Bloomington: Indiana University Press, 1987).

SPACKS, PATRICIA, *Imagining a Self: Autobiography and the Novel in Eighteenth-Century England* (Cambridge, Mass.: Harvard University Press, 1976).

STANTON, DOMNA, *The Female Autograph: the Theory and Practice of Autobiography from the Tenth to the Twentieth Century* (Chicago: University of Chicago Press, 1987).

STENDHAL, *Vie de Henri Brulard* (Paris: Gallimard, Bibliothèque de la Pléiade, 1955).

STERN, DANIEL, *Mes Souvenirs* (Paris: Calmann Lévy, 1977).

STURROCK, JOHN, *The Language of Autobiography; Studies in the First Person Singular* (Cambridge: Cambridge University Press, 1993).

TRISTAN, FLORA, *Les Pérégrinations d'une paria* (Paris: F. Maspero, 1980).

WOOLF, VIRGINIA, *A Room of One's Own* (London: HarperCollins, Flamingo, 1994).

INDEX